I'll Walk Again

by

Esther Loewen Vogt

and

Paul D. Miller

*With Introduction
by
Bishop McFerrin Stowe*

HERALD PRESS, SCOTTDALE, PENNSYLVANIA
1972

To
Today's youth
Who search for the way to walk

"I can do all things
through Christ
which strengtheneth me"

(Philippians 4:13).

Preface

Sometimes God locks our feet into paths He wants us to take so that we can't stray from them. I had just completed my fourth novel and was dibbling mentally for a fifth plot. Nothing jelled.

Then a phone call came from Peabody, Kansas, eighteen miles from my home, which was to make a divine impact on my life.

At the time I had never heard of Paul D. Miller — "Reverend Paul," as he is affectionately called — and when he asked if I would listen to a story he had to tell, my writer's itch pricked with anticipation. I rushed around and set the living room to rights, threw a casserole into the oven for lunch, and paused long enough to rearrange my hair.

When he limped up the front walk half an hour later and I listened spellbound to his dynamic story I realized why no plot had jelled for me. Without a doubt this was to be my next writing project!

As Paul Miller's story unfolded in the weeks and months that followed, I began to realize why God brought him out of an obscure childhood into the light of His service. For his depth, his keen spiritual perception, and warm, compassionate nature have molded him into the kind of personality which endears him to everyone with whom he comes in contact. This is a story of courage, in the face of poverty, pain, and fear. It is also the story of a faith so vibrant and so thrilling that it has in itself been a great lesson to me. Yet in spite of his obtuse background, Paul Miller's story is peppered generously with witty incidents and salted with his ability to laugh at his own mistakes.

It has been a challenge and a joy to work with "Reverend Paul" and his lovely wife Marilyn on this book, and it is with deep humility and appreciation that I have written down the words of this life story.

It is impossible to separate and acknowledge my indebtedness to everyone who contributed to the contents. I can only set down what I have learned so that others too may know God is actively at work in hearts and lives of men today in order to fulfill His purpose. That to "walk again" emotionally, spiritually, and physically is God's gift to man; and that those who read this life story may claim Paul's motto: "I can do all things through Christ which strengtheneth me."

Esther Loewen Vogt

Foreword

"The woods are lovely, dark and deep,
But I have promises to keep,
And miles to go before I sleep,
*And miles to go before I sleep."**

These words from Robert Frost's poem, "Stopping by Woods on a Snowy Evening," have special meaning to me since my accident in December 1966. And I am grateful to God for allowing me to walk a few more miles with my wife, children, and friends. When I look back over the Lord's guidance in my life, I feel ashamed that my life has not been more radiant and that my faith has not been a more contagious thing. I receive a great blessing when I tell what the Lord Jesus Christ has done for me, and it is with a prayer in my heart that I tell the story again. And as I tell it I trust that others will receive a blessing as they discover that Jesus is still alive and working in lives of men today.

Paul D. Miller

*From *Complete Poems of Robert Frost.* Copyright 1949 by Holt, Rinehart, and Winston. Used by permission.

Introduction

It was right after Christmas in 1966 when word came to me that one of my preachers was dying as a result of a large spotlight falling from a balcony and striking him on the head. That minister was the Reverend Paul Miller — but he refused to die. In the hospital they told me that if he should live he would never walk again, that he would never talk again. But on Easter Sunday 1967, with the help of a cane, Paul walked into his pulpit and preached the resurrection, the story of God's love and God's power.

One might say that Paul was lucky, but some of us who watched this drama of life and death found something bigger than luck, something greater than chance. We saw the providence of God. But this is the story of this young man's life that is told in this book, and each one who reads it must decide for himself whether the terrible and wonderful things that have happened to Paul Miller reveal the providence of a loving Father.

This is the fascinating story of a baby born in a one-room log cabin in Cook Branch in Wolfe County, Kentucky. One might paraphrase a question asked of another baby born in an unlikely place — Bethlehem in Judah: "Can anything good come out of Cook Branch?"

The answer is one I want to give: Yes, a splendid young minister of the United Methodist Church, who is loved by his people and who ministers in a fine way; a young man whose life may help us answer another question: "Do you believe in miracles?" You may decide that his life gives a strong affirmative answer.

Bishop W. McFerrin Stowe
The United Methodist Church
Topeka, Kansas

Contents

BOOK ONE *"Woods"*

1

"Git 'em, Ollie! Ketch that lizard!" I yelled as I dove under an apex of sagging, broken boards that had once been a corncrib. I heard my tattered jeans rip again.

My young uncle Ollie pushed the yellow hair out of his freckled face and scrambled among the hodgepodge of rotting timber and grunted. His shaggy head suddenly reappeared as he shook himself.

"He got clean away," he panted. "What in tarnation do ya'll want with them lizards, Chester? If you want them so bad, why don't you ketch 'em yourself?"

"Yeah, why don't you?" I echoed.

My other uncle, Chester, narrowed his eyes and wrinkled his short red nose. "Aw, come off it," he drawled, and clamped his lips together tightly.

Earl, my scrawny brother, hiked up his dirty dun-colored trouser legs and squatted down on an old rotted beam. Then he picked up a dried grass-blade and slapped it between his teeth.

The warm summer sun dipped into Cook Branch and glinted off the white sandstone cliffs to the east and threw a muted shadowy pattern on Earl's long tangled hair. He spat out the blade of grass.

"*Green* lizards, Ollie. Me an' Chester figgered to have some fun racin' them," he said finally.

"Race them!" I exploded. My brother and I rarely agreed on things. "Well, you two kin count me out. I'm

15

a-goin' to the house. You three kin — '' I lunged forward. Too late I saw a rusty nail half-hidden in one of the broken boards that lay on the ground. I felt it crunch into my big toe and I screamed as it reappeared just above the nail.

Agonizing pain shot into my foot and I sank to the ground, gasping in short sobbing breaths.

Horrified, Earl and my two young uncles stared at my toe. I tugged frantically at the board, but each jerk sent chills of pain slashing along my spine. I worked the board this way and that until I finally pulled my foot free. I don't know why they didn't help me, for I was younger. Apparently they figured a five-year-old hillbilly lad should be able to take care of himself.

"Better git into the house and let Mom put some salve on it," Earl said diffidently.

Painfully I struggled to my feet. Fire jabbed in my foot as I inched along, and I drew up my leg and hopped toward the one-roomed log cabin we called "home."

My father was a sharecropper on the hillsides of Wolfe County, Kentucky, who tried to eke out a living, raising tobacco and corn on the sloping hillsides. The land belonged to Grandpa and Grandma Dunn who lived a half mile up the "holler" in a two-roomed cabin. Our farming equipment consisted of several hoes, a broken-down old mule, a single-bottom plow, a walking single-bladed cultivator, and an old homemade sled. A gentle brindle cow, a handful of squawking chickens, and a struggling garden completed our farming enterprises.

Mud-chinking had fallen out between the logs of the

cabin and left gaps where splinters of sunlight needled their way through the roughhewn logs. The walls papered with mail order catalog pages crackled in the hot wind. Windowless, the cabin was stifling in the summer heat and freezing in the wintertime.

I was born in this cabin on August 16, 1932, escorted by a hefty midwife who had clumped down the mountain path for the impending occasion.

My parents with their three children slept in the cabin's single room on crude, homemade beds, made bearable with feather mattresses. Mom did the cooking in a wide, crumbling fireplace, and her "laundromat" consisted of a huge black kettle over an open fire in the woodyard. She thrust slivers of homemade lye soap into the kettle and when the water bubbled and sudsed she tossed in our tattered clothes. Then she strung them on bushes along Wolfe Creek to dry.

The outhouse, filled with corncobs and old Sears Roebuck catalogs, sat across the "crick" above which was our well and only water supply. We boys were saddled with the never-ending chore of keeping the water bucket filled, lugging in every drop of water the family used, and hauling in firewood from the hills.

Except during a rainy spell, Wolfe Creek ran dry. In these dry seasons we used the creekbed as a road; otherwise we followed the footpath that marched boldly along the sloping spur of the creek. Flanked by scarlet laurel and the aromatic pink rhododendron the path meandered past a tangle of blackberry bushes and wild plum thickets. We picked blackberries, blueberries, and huckleberries in summertime which Mom canned for use in the long winter months.

Now as I stumbled up the dirt path that led to the cabin door, I was scarcely aware of the scrawny tobacco acres clinging to the hillside. The Kentucky Appalachians cast long violet shadows over Cook Branch as Mom turned away from her cooking pots over the fireplace.

"What's done come over you, Paul?" she asked from the doorway, her hands sticky from stirring up the inevitable batch of baking powder biscuits.

"I — stepped on a — n-nail!" I wailed.

Without a word she wiped her hands on her gravy-stained apron and went to her "yarb" shelf. She reached for liniment and Rosebud salve, and rescued a scrap of dirty linen from a box in one corner, and bound up my toe.

For days I sat disconsolately in the cabin doorway, flinching with the throbbing that never quite subsided in my foot. Even the sound of drying bean pods rattling against the eaves didn't tempt me to ask Mom for my favorite dish of ham hock, bacon grit with beans, and cream gravy.

Sometimes the day was soft with the sun flowing like honey along the hillsides; the next it trembled as hot winds rushed through the woods in gusts, blowing into the chinks of the cabins and whistling eerie, tuneless bars of sound.

My foot began to swell as the pain increased, and the leg grew ugly and discolored. I cried most of the time. What was worse, we were miles from the nearest doctor.

On the third day Mom made up her mind. "Paul, you're too big to carry. I'm a-goin' to take you to Lee

City to see the missionary lady. Maybe she has some-thin' to take away your hurtin'."

"Some day I'll walk again," I said thickly as I watched her hitch the old mule to the sled. Then she half-carried me outdoors and placed me on the rough wooden seat of the sled. She clucked to the old mule and the sled moved slowly down the dry creekbed, each jouncing, jogging movement sending unbearable jabs of pain down my leg. The three-mile trip seemed interminable.

Suddenly the church spire hove into sight and we reached the little village with its single feedstore, grocery store, blacksmith shop, the church, and a smattering of houses in various stages of disrepair. We lumbered past the little store where we regularly traded eggs for salt, sugar, flour, baking powder, and other staples.

Now we stopped beside the missionary's neat white frame house. It sat back pertly from the board-walk and whitewashed gate, with bright pink holly-hocks nodding over the fence.

Miss Madge Carter, the short, stocky white-haired missionary, welcomed us warmly and led us inside. The gay curtains on the shiny windows and colored check-ered cloth on the kitchen table caught my eye in spite of my agonizing pain, for somehow everything seemed so clean, so livable here, and a yearning in my heart stirred me.

Softly and capably she moved, cleaning out my wound and dabbing ointments and antiseptics over my toe, and then bandaged it with fresh gauze.

"Before you go," she said after she had snipped off

the last bit of adhesive, "would it be all right if I read some Scripture and had a word of prayer?"

Mom nodded, and the missionary read thrilling words from a black Book. And then she prayed, her face shining with faith, and somehow I knew that the Friend to whom she was talking was listening.

We visited her several times after that to change the dressings until my toe was healed. Each time she read the Bible and prayed. The last time we came I looked up into her kind, gentle face and a rush of warmth and love spilled over me. I blurted out, unthinking:

"Ma'am, some day I'm gonna be a preacher!"

Little did I know the effect these words would have upon my life, and the depths into which I would be drawn as a result.

2

"We're a-goin' a-move; we're a-goin' a-move today!" My older sister Evalee chanted in singsong fashion, her dirty green dress swirling over her skinny knees as she danced in front of the cabin.

We were all more than a little excited, for the log cabin had become too cramped for our growing family which had by now increased to six. Time and weather had taken toll of the dirty hovel and now it sagged bleak and tired on its rugged hillside.

A half mile down the "holler" a little yellow frame house perched unoccupied on a clay bank. A wide-branched apple tree stood guard in the front.

The time was 1937, and I was almost six. Surely, we were climbing up the social ladder, for the frame house was fully twice the size of the log cabin. It boasted of two rooms: the larger being combination kitchen, dining and bedroom; the other one, ironically enough, a storeroom for our annual corn crop!

In the front yard sat our pride and joy — a real well, complete with bucket and rope. Earl and I heaved a big sigh of relief, for now our long, tedious water-lugging treks would be over.

Down the slope stood a fair-sized old barn. One room could be used as a tobacco shed, while the other had been converted into living quarters for some kin: an uncle, aunt, and their three children claimed

School days at Clarksville, Ohio. Paul D. Miller, a sixth grader, is fourth from left in front row.

Mrs. Carl (Rhoda) Miller holding Paul and his sister Evalee sitting on the steps of their one-room log cabin in Kentucky. Photo by Madge Carter.

The frame house at Cook Branch where the family moved from the log cabin. It burned when Paul and Earl were playing with matches. Photo by Madge Carter.

Evalee, Paul, and Elma Miller on Pancho, Dayton, Ohio.

Paul about age sixteen with his mother and sister Pat in Ohio.

Carl and Rhoda (Dunn) Miller, 1953, parents of Paul D. Miller.

24

squatters' rights there. It would be fun to play with Cousins Charles and Eugene every day.

"You orter see them crawdads a-swimmin' in the ol' mudhole," Charles told us importantly, and our necks pricked with excitement.

Pant legs rolled up to our knees, we hung over the muddy creek bank and angled for the wriggling creatures that darted around in the slimy green water.

It was almost as much fun as playing with the doodlebugs on the stone cliffs. *That* was another real Huck Finn-ish pastime. We'd creep silently among the crumbly white rocks looking for doodlebug holes. Gathering around the holes we'd chant:

"Doodlebug, doodlebug,

Will you come up?"

And the person whose bug surfaced first was eligible to make a wish.

"I wish. . . ."

I wonder how often we wished for more satisfying meals, for better clothes, for automobiles like "rich folks." Now and then we'd see old Chevys and Fords chugging down the holler, the people always well dressed (in our inexperienced eyes). Presumably they were headed toward Dayton, Ohio, mecca of all that spelled weath and prosperity.

As adventuresome boys we dared almost anything. There were the times we snuck behind the barn, and as many red-blooded Americans have attempted through the ages, tried our hand at smoking.

Except that instead of real tobacco — of which our shed reeked pungently — we dried the long, silvery leaves of the "life everlasting" weed, crumbled into powder, rolled thumb-and-fingerfuls into a precious bit of brown paper, and puffed. I doubt that we might have become addicted to anything resembling nicotine, for the weed tasted horrible. It was probably more for daring than pleasure that we indulged in the practice at all. One thing we feared was that Mom would find out about our "sin," and tan our hides with her sturdy willow switches which she did often.

Sometimes we hunched over a circle crudely drawn on the ground and played marbles. The agates, cat's-eye and multicolored, were poured out of tobacco pouches onto the ground. The game lasted until a fight broke out and then we'd quit.

Religious life in the hills was often watered down with making moonshine and other less-than-moral practices. Yet a mountain funeral could usually bring out a person's most reverent feelings.

When my Aunt Cordie died, grief tramped the narrow hillsides, for it was my first experience with death. Gaunt mountaineers fashioned a coffin of rough pine boards, while womenfolk dressed her quiet form in her best starched blue cotton with a bunch of wild violets tucked over her lifeless bosom.

Evalee wept openly. "Aunt Cordie's daid!"

I wondered at the copious tears that flowed and the sad, tragic faces that bent over for a last look at the departed.

On the hillside graveyard the hole waited wide-mouthed for its silent tenant. As we marched dolorously up the stony path behind the grim-faced pallbearers I couldn't help but wonder if Aunt Cordie would feel the cold winds that swept over the mountains in the wintertime, or the warm summer showers beating upon the sodden mound. Maybe the pine-scented mountain breeze whispering through the heavily laden apple boughs would keep her company, and maybe her big, sad eyes would look happy now.

Mom and Evalee's arms were laden with wild flowers and I was glad. Surely Aunt Cordie wouldn't mind the lonely hill so much, smothered with fragrant laurel and lulled by soughing pines.

The circuit preacher apparently wasn't available to conduct the burial service, so a tall, rugged mountaineer whose dormant religion stirred with life muttered verses from the Bible:

"Yea, though I walk through the valley of the shadow of death, I will fear no evil. . . . Surely goodness and mercy shall follow me. . . ." And the inevitable gospel hymns that rolled somberly from uninhibited voices:

"Tell Mother I'll be there, in answer to her prayer. . . ."

I heard the clink of stone against shovel as dirt was thrown over the lowered coffin, and saw the flowers heaped upon the mound — soft pink petals already browning in the hot summer wind. In childish despair I turned away.

What would it be like to die? Years later I was to have a personal encounter with the grim specter, for Death stalked me and sought me out more than once. But for now, it was enough to realize Aunt Cordie was gone — and would never return.

My grandparents, the O. L. Dunns, lived down one

fork of the hollow and a favorite pastime was a visit to Grandma.

I can see her yet, a gray, elfin figure moving among the rock-bordered paths of her flower garden: gay pink hollyhocks, stately purple larkspur, a blaze of cosmos, and fringes of marigolds all marching in a riot of color around the two-roomed mountain shack; yellow butterflies, silver dust on their wings, winnowing down to cling to the sun-drenched blossoms, then whirring away, with wings fanning.

Inside the cabin the smell of potatoes baking on the hot coals in the fireplace made my mouth water. Peeled and buttered, they oozed with the delicious aroma of nature's best.

Between the two rooms there was a narrow pantry. High up were bunklike beds, and it was fun to sleep in the thick feather ticks, listening to the chirrup-chirrup of crickets at night. Sometimes we crouched down and watched the moon, orange and enormous, spin across the heavens with a trail of splintered diamonds in its wake. And night, once the fire died, seemed to stretch out like wet rawhide.

One hot summer day Earl and I grew restless. Earlier we'd played in the woods, watching a mother bobwhite with her flock of chicks clucking across our path, and scurrying into the bushes like brown leaves before an autumn wind.

For a while I gazed up at a hawk soaring in long, easy circles into the bright blue sky. I plucked a blade of Johnson grass and held it between my teeth and blew on it. It sounded almost like a hawk. except hoarser. I tried to catch a bumblebee in a jar, but it buzzed away. No fun.

That's when I got an idea. "Let's play with matches," I said brashly.

Earl glanced at me out of the corner of his eye. "Matches? Mom's gonna tan our hides good if she ketches us."

"Aw, she won't have to find out. We'll go somewhere whar she cain't see us," I drawled.

For a moment Earl cocked his head and contemplated. "Sure. Let's go into the corncrib room. She won't look thar."

He tiptoed into the dining-kitchen-bedroom and grabbed a handful of matches from the old Clabber Girl baking powder tin and we slipped into the corncrib.

Scratch-strike . . . I loved the odor of sulphur as the match burst into flame. Just how it happened I'll never know. Perhaps our boyish prank simply made us more careless than usual. For one minute the bright blue fire blazed red, and then suddenly it became a sheet of solid flame.

"Fire!"

With a cry I stumbled back into our living quarters. Mom, bent over the big stone butter churn, thumped away rhythmically. Then she caught sight of the flaming corncrib through the open door, grabbed her bowl of finished butter, and dashed outside. Earl was at her heels.

I cowered beside the bed, feeling guilty and afraid. What had I done? Our yellow frame house was burning!

Already smoke rushed into the living quarters and

I began to cough. The fire crackled as tongues of flame licked at the doorjamb, but I remained transfixed as I watched the fire creep steadily closer.

Then I heard Mom's anguished screams behind me. "Paul . . . are you in thar?"

She reached out for my hand and dragged me outside into the fresh air. I sputtered and coughed, my eyes burning from the smoke.

Helplessly we watched the hungry fire devour the yellow frame structure, together with its meager contents. A dark cloud of smoke, shot with angry flames, rolled into the blue sky. Dad, Mom, and the four of us youngsters stood horrified as the smoke billowed from black to gray to shimmering pale wisps of nothing.

The old mule stood with sharp ears cocked in the nearby pasture; the Red Rock hens scratched and cackled in the yellow clay earth as though nothing had happened. But the old apple tree on the baked clay bank bowed forlorn and grim with its cloak of browned leaves.

All that we had saved were the ragged clothes we wore — and Mom's salvaged bowl of yellow butter.

3

Homeless and heavyhearted, we gathered under the brown old apple tree for a family council. What should we do now? There were no more houses or cabins available in the hollow, and we could definitely not afford to rebuild.

Mom came from a family of thirteen children, of whom several had left the mountains to make their way in Dayton, Ohio.

Occasionally they had returned to Kentucky for a visit, looking prosperous and worldly-wise in unpatched store-bought clothes, and wearing shoes with both heels intact and soles without holes. Even shoelaces were genuine and not cut from a length of twine.

What really sold us on our kins' affluency, I think, was the cars — shabby but real. Earl and I stood bug-eyed whenever the old Chevys and Fords, wired together for convenience, would rattle up the narrow mountain roads. It was decidedly a more comfortable mode of transportation than jogging down the dry bed of Wolfe Creek via mule sled.

Dad was facing us now, still listing the pros and cons of leaving the hills.

"I'm all fer goin'," Earl popped up boldly. "Think of the long ride in a otty-mobeel!"

Mom nodded. "It might be kinda excitin', livin' in the city."

Of course, we all loved "the holler," and saying good-bye to Cook Branch wouldn't be easy.

But once the decision was made to leave, we needed only to beg a ride to Dayton for ourselves. Since we were bereft of all physical belongings there was nothing to pack.

Once more we bumped and jostled down the hard, dry creekbed, and soon left the hills behind us.

The two days' journey wasn't without incident, for we stopped more than once to patch the paper-thin tires and to eat. For our meals we drew up before some corner grocery, purchased a sturdy length of bologna, and a couple of loaves of "boughten bread," and maybe a few bananas, and pulled over to a shady side of the street and feasted. This was sumptuous fare compared to our steady diet of cornbread, biscuits, rabbit, and squirrel.

For the first several days we stayed with our relatives until Dad found a place to live.

"It's a brick buildin', an' sets near the tracks," he told us with a male's off-handed unconcern. We immediately visioned a comfortable lodging set in the midst of the hustle and bustle of the city.

Somehow we weren't quite prepared for the long, shabby brick cleft in the strata of a Negro ghetto. Grimy and smoke-stained, the slummy three-storied apartment house sat next to the sidewalk. A dirty, unkempt alley crawled behind it where rats and other vermin stole their gray shapes into littered doorways. Sour-smelling taverns and filthy, unpainted shops straggled down the uneven streets like veins with ugly ulcer sores.

Again we were herded into two dingy, musty rooms. One of our chief sports was to rush into the kitchen at night, jerk the pull chain that dangled from a single naked bulb overhead, and watch the cockroaches and rats scurry for cover!

Dad had found work in the GH&R Foundry, and so we settled into our new way of life without fanfare. I was seven years old now, and as the hot August days dragged into September we were marched off to Washington Elementary School, about seven or eight blocks away. We were almost the only white students in our classrooms.

Because the school situation became practically intolerable at times, Earl and I played hooky every chance we got, hiding in the empty boxcars that rusted on the nearby railroad tracks. When school was out we'd hurry on home. But the gang often met us at the railroad bridge and beat us up.

"Yah, Yah! Fight 'em, Earl!" someone would yell, and they'd set my brother and me against each other. Our fraternal fights apparently became the gang's pet sport. Nearly every day we'd stumble home from school, beaten up by our tormentors.

One day after Earl had donned his coveted first new pair of dungarees and *whole* shoes, the gang descended on us after school as usual. They made short work of his new duds. He came home in tatters.

We had to plan a new strategy to outwit them.

"Tomorrow let's come home from school another way," Earl suggested. "Let's cross over the railroad overpass and mebbe we kin get away from those guys thataway."

We stole quietly through the bushes that clung to the incline leading toward the bridge and tried to slip behind the tall poles. But the boys anticipated our move and waited for us. They told us to drop down from the overpass. Apparently they hoped to attack us behind the wall without trouble. We pretended ignorance.

"Show us how you-uns want us to do it," I said innocently.

Their fingers clinging to the side of the cement wall, they prepared to drop down to the tracks below.

"Now!" Earl shouted, and both he and I jumped up and down on fingers that were still exposed to our sight.

"Ow-ow-ow!"

You could hear their yells for blocks up the shimmering tracks as we stomped on those knuckles!

Then I yelled loud enough for them to hear. "Le's go back under the bridge."

We saw them scurry under the bridge to meet us. Instead, we dropped off the wall and raced home, laughing all the way.

If a certain kind-faced, heavyset black girl named Martha hadn't taken our side against them and protected us from time to time. I wonder what finally would have happened. I think we were eternally grateful to her for helping us against our tormentors.

Prowling through the alleys, Earl and I were lucky now and then to find broken, cast-off toys in someone's trash can. Sometimes we also discovered thrown-out food behind a grocery store and we'd have a feast. Invariably we also picked up something else: the infernal, scabby skin infection known as *impetigo!* We were rarely without the constantly itching crust while we lived in the ghetto.

One day Earl and I wandered down a shabby side street when I caught sight of two rather drab-looking Indian dolls lying carelessly on the porch of a disreputable shack.

"Look, Earl," I cried excitedly, "I reckon nobody wants them Injun dolls. Why don't we-uns take 'em?"

Earl shrugged his thin shoulders. "Sure. Why not?"

But when we came home and Mom caught sight of them, her eyes shot sparks.

"Lissen here, you two. Whar'd you get them dolls? I want a straight answer."

After we confessed that we'd stolen them she marched us firmly back to the shack where we returned the dolls and sweated through an abject apology to the woman who lived there. Of course, the willow stitch routine followed when we got home.

We never had a dime to spend; so for a short time I entertained the men in one of the taverns with a sort of shuffling tap dance for whatever they paid me. The men, lolling over their drinks in the dingy bar, clapped their hands and scooped small change from their pockets and gave it to me.

This kept me in pocket money — until one day a policeman walked through the tavern door and tapped his nightstick on my shoulder.

"Beat it, kid," he said sternly. "And don't ever let me catch you in here again!"

Life in the ghetto battered us down. Mexicans, working on the railroad, frequented the taverns, and often Mom was forced to pick up her broom and chase away the drunks that lounged in our doorway. Once we watched a Mexican and a Negro in a gruesome fight. We turned away nauseated after the black man lay dead in a pool of blood beside our doorstep.

I was very young, but I remember thinking one day, after witnessing the seamy side of our neighborhood: "Is this all life is for?" Yet I was far too young to think of trying to change things.

We moved out of the ghetto into a dirty gray shack on the other side of the city. My brother Earl and I still took our disagreements out on each other with our fists.

After one such rough bout I landed hard against the flat-topped coal heater. With a howl of excruciating pain I tried to straighten up. The damage was done. An ugly red burn seared across my abdomen which took weeks of sulphur salve treatment to heal. I carry the scar to this day.

It was about at this time that an itinerant photographer knocked on our door, leading a small brown pony behind him.

"Ma'am," he said decisively to our mother, "You have some likely-looking kids over there. Why don't you let me take pictures of that one" — he pointed to me — "sitting astride my little Pancho? It's a sight you'll never forget." Nor have I ever forgotten, for the picture is among my cherished possessions today.

When we transported our meager belongings to the east side of Dayton we inherited the inevitable stockyard stench and the pungent odor of an ammonia factory on either side of us.

One of the highlights of this neighborhood, as I recall, was the nearby chewing gum factory. The lip-smacking scent of "juicy fruit" hung over the place like a pall, and Earl and I roamed this territory hopefully.

Hope changed to luck one day when we discovered a huge chunk of uncut gum, fully the size of a cake of ice.

"Wouldya look at that!" Earl whistled. "Wow! Gum — gobs of it!"

"Shall we-uns lug it home?" I asked, drooling at the sight.

"Nope," Earl said sagely. "If Mom finds out we'd get whaled for sartin. Better hide it in them bushes over thar." And that's where the hunk of chewing gum stayed until we had "chawed" it to mouthfuls of flavorless gray pulp.

One day when another kid and I were fighting near the gum factory he lit out after me. I made a beeline for the street. Too late I heard the honking horn and screeching brakes and felt the thud as the car hit me. My leg crumpled under me and blood oozed over my face from the cut on my head. The street squeezed into a narrow blur of nausea, and the pain and tears made a sort of kaleidoscope of people and traffic around me. I struggled to remain conscious. Presently there was the wail of a siren and someone was lifting me into an ambulance and then we screamed toward the hospital.

Hours later I was wheeled into the ward, my leg a stiff white sculptured mass of pain, and my head throbbing under a gigantic turban bandage.

For several weeks I lay in that hospital bed, unable to get up.

One day Pat Bauer, a bachelor from the insurance company covering the accident, visited me. He began to take a personal interest in me, usually coming loaded with bananas and candy and other goodies.

The day he brought me a windup toy (my first) which crawled all over the stiff white mountain of my leg, I could grin again

"Hey, you're swell!" I told Pat gratefully.

He grinned and slapped my shoulder, "Know something, Paul? You're a pretty good kid yourself. When I die, I'll leave everything I have to you."

I knew he was quite wealthy but for a while I clung to that brash promise. Later on he was married and promptly forgot the words he spoke to me that day.

But I never forgot. I remembered what nagged at the back of my mind earlier: "Is this all there is to life?" Poverty, filth, hunger, gloom, despair, and the stigma of being "poor white trash.". . .

Someday, somehow, I knew I must walk out of my stultifying surroundings and rise above the constant physical and spiritual poverty wherein fate had thrust me. But it was to take years before I was able to shake off the shackles of my confining bonds.

4

We moved to Clarksville when I was about ten years old. This rural Ohio town lay some forty miles southeast of Dayton. Dad maintained his job with the GH&R Foundry, living in Dayton and commuting home during holidays and weekends. We had become attached to this rural community on earlier visits to Aunt Laura and Uncle Bernie, and of course it reminded us of our beloved Appalachian Mountains with its wooded hills and sloping meadows.

The house, small but sturdy, boasted three rooms and a basement. It sat almost astride a hill about three miles from town. In the deep, cold well we kept our milk and butter sweet and our Jell-O solid.

An old abandoned streetcar on the yard became a bedroom for Earl and me. One thing which stands out indelibly in my mind about these remote sleeping quarters was the yellow jackets' nesting in the walls. Earl and I delighted in disturbing the wasps and when they buzzed out angrily we ducked under the bed-covers, howling with laughter. Occasionally our chuckles turned into tears.

The house nestled near a secluded woods that thrived in wild blackberries, mulberries, raspberries, strawberries, and dewberries. Hazelnut and walnut groves provided nutting parties for us. We spent hours cracking nuts with a hammer on a smooth, shiny stone.

One morning Mom handed us several lard pails. "I want you kids to go berryin' today. Just don't eat too many!" she added tartly.

Earl wore his new gay red cap as we set out into the bright June morning. Sunlight made warm freckles everywhere as it slanted through a tangle of pine boughs and live oak. Overhead sounded the wheezy call of flycatchers and sassy blue jays.

Our pails were almost brimful when Earl accidently stepped into a hornets' nest. This time he didn't laugh. With a yowl he rushed through the bushes, upsetting pails and spilling berries as he ran. I saw the flash of red as his cap sailed through the air — and then I heard a splash. Earl had dived into the creek to escape the stingers. We lost buckets, berries, cap and all that day. But we trembled most because we knew we'd have to reckon with Mom's willow switch.

Each day a rickety yellow school bus stopped for us. Because Dad boarded away from home during the week his paycheck didn't quite reach to clothe us properly. We still went to school in rags and with torn scraps of leather on our feet.

"You're nuthin' but poor white trash!" the boys would jeer, and I'd feel like crawling into a hole and dragging it in after me.

There never was quite enough money for things like pencils and tablets, and gifts to exchange at Christmastime. When other kids drew names, like as not there were smothered giggles because we didn't have the means to be a part of it. We never got leading roles in school plays, or invitations to nice kids' parties either.

"Poor white trash" kids lived with their folks in cramped, dingy houses which smelled of cabbage and pork, bean soup and corn bread, and wet clothes and matted dirt. I realized all this, and it nauseated me. And there was nothing I could do about it. No wonder I began hating it all. Again, I wondered if life was always to be this way.

In spite of berries and vegetables from our garden which Mom canned endlessly, there never seemed to be enough milk for all of us. So when a farmer who lived down the hill near the railroad tracks offered me a job for all the skim milk we could drink I was forced to accept it. I did my share of work in the fields, plowing and disking, and helping with the haying.

Dad had sunk many a paycheck into old cars. When he had rattled home with them, they shuddered, heaved, and died. Of course, after he took them apart they sometimes redeemed themselves partly as junk.

One summer morning before he left for work he took Earl and me aside.

"Boys, that old '32 Chevy a-sittin' on top of the hill past the woodyard is ready to junk. I want you to start strippin' it today."

I guess there were worse things to do than tearing old cars apart. With an abundance of shade and the day mellow and lazy, Earl and I slammed wrenches and hammers as we dismantled the old heap piece by piece.

After a period of our intermittent clanking noises, I looked up. A stooped, scrawny man trudged up the hill, his face dark and unshaven and his clothes looking like refugees from a rag factory.

"Look, Earl!" I cried, pointing with a greasy finger, "somebody's comin' up the hill an' he sure looks like a filthy ol' tramp!"

Earl whistled. "Boy, are you kiddin'. Maybe we oughtta hightail it out of here afore he decides to get mean."

My brother Earl usually knew best although I didn't always want to admit it. We started to sneak down the hill when the man spotted us.

"Hey, you! Don't you young'uns know me? I'm your ma's brother."

"Uncle J. H.!" I shrieked. "Well, I sure didn't reckonize y'all."

Earl chuckled. "Wait 'til Mom sees you. Bet she'd have a fit."

"Hey, that's an idea," Uncle J.H. said. "Don't make so much noise, and let's talk it over real quiet-like. Why don't I play like I'm chasin' you two and you start hollerin'? Then when your ma comes out of the house, let's lay it on real thick."

We fell in with his plans. He pretended to chase us around the remains of the old Chev and we screamed and yelled as though all the demons of hell were after us.

Mom marched up the hill like a provost marshal to see what was going on. When she saw the dark-faced stranger chasing us she grabbed the ax from the nearby woodyard and took out after him. Mom had never been afraid of anything and she wasn't now.

At first we boys thought it was funny. But when we realized how serious she was about catching our "pursuer" we grew alarmed.

"Stop it, Mom!" Earl shouted. "It's Uncle J.H. — your brother."

"Mom — don't!" I howled in fright.

But our voices were lost to her in her determination to overpower the man and she grabbed him roughly by his arms and threw him to the ground.

"I'll larn you to rough up my young'uns!" she snarled, standing over him with the ax raised.

I cried again. "Mom — don't! It's your brother!"

He muttered thickly. "Rhodie — Rhodie — he's right. I *am* J.H. —"

She paused midway in her deliberate action and froze.

"J. — H. — my brother? Oh, my God. . . ." Limply she dropped the ax to the ground.

After he had washed the soot from his face (he wasn't unshaven after all) and sat down to a plateful of cold watermelon, our uncle finally stopped shaking. And so did the rest of us!

When I was about eleven, Bill Hiles offered me a job as general helper on his farm. The Hiles were an elderly German couple. From the very beginning the short, portly little German with the John L. Lewis eyebrows called me "Pee Wee," and we hit it off well together. During the summer months I worked every day; while school was in session I went to their farm on Fridays after school and stayed until Sunday night. I was paid the munificent wage of fifty cents per day, plus all I could eat. Sometimes I wondered if they didn't get the wrong end of the deal, since Mrs. Hiles was an outstanding cook. For the first time in my life I could eat all I wanted!

A part of my job was to transplant tobacco seedlings from the hotbeds into neat, even rows down in the bottoms. Later the plants needed to be hoed, topped, dewormed, and tended until ready for harvest. Then we cut the large plants, stuck them on tobacco sticks, and hauled them up the hill. Pulled by Jack and Kate, the team of stubborn mules, the wagon creaked and lumbered up the slope, and then we hung the tobacco in the barn to dry. During the winter months we graded it and prepared it for market.

One day while I was deworming the tobacco plants I noticed an ugly big tobacco worm leering at me, just *begging* to be decapitated.

"OK," I muttered. "You done asked for it, Worm!"

WHAM! My corn knife descended. Unfortunately I missed the Wicked Worm and hit my wrist. The white scar on my right wrist is still mute evidence of my unceremonious encounter with a tobacco worm!

Mr. Hiles also raised the most luscious watermelons in the county. Railroad section hands working the tracks often yielded to temptation and helped themselves. We'd find empty, red-rimmed rinds strewn along the ditches nearly every day during the watermelon season.

My boss had enough of this thieving and decided to teach the snitchers a lesson. He cut out a small chunk of rind and injected croton oil into the melons that grew nearest the tracks, then replaced the plugs. Apparently the croton oil proved to be extremely laxative, much to the hands' dismay!

44

One day when Dad was home, he and I walked along the tracks together. He drew a plug of tobacco from his pouch and popped it into his mouth. I watched his jaws work rhythmically as he enjoyed his "chaw" (the way his mother before him had) and noticed the brown juice dribble down his chin and spot the front of his dirty blue shirt.

"Dad," I said impulsively, "how about givin' me a 'chaw'?"

Dad looked at me intently. "Naw, Paul. I reckon I better not."

"Please? I'm almost growed up now — " I stretched myself to my full height. "I'm a reg'lar hired hand, you know."

He deliberated for a few minutes, then drew out his pouch again and dropped a "chaw-sized" hunk into my outstretched palm.

At last I can prove I'm a man, I thought, and placed the plug between my teeth. Somehow I managed to swallow it. Very unmanlike, I became violently ill, and crouched beside the tracks, retching and heaving until I had dispelled the raw substance. That put a crimp into my tobacco habit. I've never picked it up since.

For days Mom had staggered around the house, her body heavy with her ninth and last child. Since we had no phone and no decent means of transportation, we boys were advised that summoning the doctor to "bring the baby" was to be our job.

One night Earl and I had settled down to sleep in our streetcar bedroom when Dad roused us.

"Time to call Doc, boys," he told us bluntly.

Violet Gail Miller, sister of Paul, born during a severe thunderstorm.

We rolled out of bed, crawled into our filthy dungarees, and started up the hill.

The wind had risen like a dark-hooded figure out of the night, stormy-browed and angry, stripping the last dead leaves from the trees and hurling them frenziedly before us. Every yellowing leaf along the road whirled in a dervish dance. As the wind lashed and writhed through the timber, black clouds raced frantically across the moon, and the darkness grew oppressive. Thunder threatened, retreated defiantly, then cowered before the bitter wind.

We were glad as our neighbors' house hove into sight and we could phone for the doctor. He would come immediately, he said.

After our wearying walk through the stormy night

we fell back exhausted into our sagging beds.

An hour or so later when our new baby sister lay red and wrinkled beside Mom in the big iron double bedstead, the doctor stood back satisfactorily and wiped his hands on a grimy Turkish towel.

"Well, here she is — born during a violent gale!" he said with a tired smile. "What will you name her? Have you decided?"

Mom glanced querulously at Dad. She always liked high-sounding words.

"What do you think, Carl? Bein's as she done come to us — like Doc said — in a 'violent gale' — what if we call her — *Violet Gail?*"

And Violet Gail it was — our new baby sister, born in a storm. Something akin to life, I thought — a violent storm, grim and foreboding.

One Sunday night after I had finished my weekend's work at the Hiles' I started for home. Usually I waded across the creek, but after a heavy rain on Saturday I was forced to walk along the creek bank and cross the challenging trestle which spanned the rising water.

As I think of it now, it reminds me something of a verse from a poem by Robert Frost:

"The woods are lovely, dark and deep.
But I have promises to keep,
And miles to go before I sleep."

Miles to go — and the night was as dark as the inside of a gopher hole. Gray clouds darted across the sky line gaunt wolves slinking out of their mountain dens. Blobs of water left from the rain made erratic patterns on the muddy ground, and I hurried breathlessly through the deep woods. After making my way gingerly across the railroad bridge in the light of the waning moon I felt relieved.

Suddenly I heard footsteps behind me and I quickened my pace. I paused for a fraction of a second and cocked my head to listen. The footsteps stopped too. I rushed on, and the steps pounded behind me. I raced frantically.

Hysterically afraid, I felt goose bumps gallop along my spine, and fear became a hurting, grinding knot of misery in my stomach and left a sickish, brassy taste in my mouth. I was sure I felt someone's hot breath on my neck. Finally I stumbled onto the path leading up the bank and home.

Slipping and sliding on the muddy path I huffed and panted toward the house. Pale orange squares of lamplight beckoned as a haven of safety. When I reached our shabby little house I flung open the front door, and threw myself over the threshold.

"Someone's — follerin' me . . ." I gasped.

Dad grabbed his shotgun and a lantern and set out into the night. But as far as we could tell, there never was anyone. The haunting footsteps apparently were only figments of my overactive imagination.

Of course, there have been other times in my dark, troubled life when I felt someone was out to get me. But at the time I didn't know what it was.

5

I'll never forget one summer when we returned to Kentucky for a visit. It was an unforgettable experience. Our hearts hammered and our stomachs growled at the thought of Grandma's corn bread and squirrel gravy, and the luscious wild berries that overran every tangled corner of the "holler."

Our visit to Aunt Lorie's house on the other side of the mountain was interrupted by the news that one of her small calves had disappeared. We boys offered to look for it.

"It could'a wandered up the side of the mountain," Earl suggested sagely, "or got lost in the pasture."

Rope in hand, shirtless and barefooted, we combed the hillsides. Peering behind laurel and rhododendron clumps and briers, we finally located the calf in the hill pasture.

I tied one end of the rope around its neck, and the other end around my waist, and we started down the hill.

Panic-stricken, the wiry calf tried to break away and I fell to my knees. As I yelled and the calf bellowed, we hurtled down the mountainside together, tumbling over brambles and sharp rocks, and coming to rest almost in front of Aunt Lorie's cottage.

My stomach was still raw and bloody that night as we sat before Grandpa's old stone fireplace, and I

49

was feeling very, very sore. I thought if I could crawl up into the high bunk of the little pantry-bedroom and go to sleep I wouldn't have to move a muscle for a week.

And then Grandpa began to talk about the cave again, and mentioned the spine-chilling name of Jesse James — and I snapped suddenly to attention.

He tilted back his rough old bark-laced chair and lit his pipe. "Yup. They say the cave whar Jesse an' his gang holed out fer a spell is still hid some'eres in these hills. In one of its rooms thar's a big round stone whar they set an' gambled durin' their hideout."

Of course, we'd heard the story many times before: Jesse James was born in Missouri, and his family was ostracized because of their sympathies with the Confederacy during the Civil War. Jesse joined guerrilla forces and his reputation for reckless daring mounted. He was outlawed because of these activities in 1866, and led a band of brigands from that time until his death. It was believed they had hidden out in one of our Kentucky caves for a time, and of course, the mere idea of trying to find the cave proved exciting enough to erase any pain I might have nurtured!

Earl and I stole sidelong glance at each other. This was something we needed to talk about under cover of darkness.

"Let's uss'ns get Ollie and Chester," Earl whispered later, "an' explore the hills an' find that cave!"

Our young uncles were only too eager to join us. We collected a good supply of pine knots for torches and begged Grandma for some matches — and a lunch.

The morning we started out, great pale shawls of mist lay across the floor of the hollow, and a long band of rich warm light bent over the sloping spur of Wolfe Creek and the dew dripped and sparkled where it met the blue morning shadows.

Barefooted and loaded down with pine knots, the four of us filed Indian fashion up and down the hills, keeping our eyes peeled for a dark crevice in the mountainside which might conceal a cave opening.

As we scoured the hills we picked berries and appeased our hunger at the same time.

Suddenly Earl let out a whoop. "Hey! Don't that look like a hole right over thar?" He pointed toward a dark blob far below.

We descended *en mass* toward the crack that seemed to split the rocktorn tree-covered hillside. Partly hidden by small boulders and clumps of brush, the hole yawned into a narrow tunnel.

Excitedly we lit our pine torches and began to squeeze through the opening. Then Chester balked.

"I'm skeered. I don't wanna go in!" he grumbled.

We tried to encourage him. "Aw, c'mon, Chester. Don't be a 'fraid-cat!"

But he refused to budge.

We left him at the mouth of the cave and dove in. The long dark tunnel flickered with murky shadows as we held our pine torches high. Farther and farther into the cave we trundled, the damp, musty odor of dank moss and wet rock forever in our nostrils.

The corridor curved this way and that, branching off into small side rooms. Then we came upon a large, high cavern.

"Look at that!" Ollie shouted. "See that big round stone in the middle? Betcha this is it!" His torch threw eerie shapes on the walls, like stealthy ghost-bandits.

Sure enough, a large, circular rock centered the barren room, brooding with shadows. Was this the table where the James gang had huddled, flickering their card decks, and clinking their dice? I grew prickly with chills just thinking about it.

We explored the room from one end to the other, and searched the bare stone floor for signs of previous habitation. There wasn't too much we could find.

."Mebbe we'd better go back," Earl said after a while. "I guess this is 'bout as far as we oughtta go."

Ollie and I followed him out into the murky corridor, playing the lights of our torches back and forth. Ominous smaller black caverns angled off the sides of the dim passageways. Under the roof vast knots of bats had packed themselves together, and as our lights disturbed the creatures they flocked down by the hundreds, squeaking and darting furiously at our torches. We hurried down the nearest passage away from them and turned the corner abruptly.

"We oughta git out pretty soon," Earl said as he swung confidently ahead of us.

The steady drip-drip of water trickling over a ledge punctuated the quiet of the limestone cave, for through the dragging ages it had formed a laced, ruffled fresco in gleaming stone.

As we wandered up and down the sinuous avenue it suddenly dawned on us — *we were lost!* Somehow, somewhere we had made a wrong turn and missed our passage to the cave entrance. . . .

We turned up one avenue, desperately hoping it was the right one, only to come upon another dead end.

"If we keep goin'," Earl said stoutly, "we're bound to get out sooner or later."

Ollie muttered, "Or later," and set on ahead.

Suddenly he let out a shout. "The ceilin' up ahead's done caved in!" His words echoed down the empty aisles and died out in the darkness. Earl and I hurried toward him. A slide of rocks had fallen down and closed our escape route!

"Lemme — push. . . ." Ollie grunted, tugging a huge slab of crumbled stone. It heaved, then fell back, pinning him against the side of the tunnel.

By this time we were thoroughly frightened. I screamed, and Earl joined me, but our cries were mere ripples of mocking laughter in the maze of lonely, winding corridors. . . .

"If only Chester kin hear us," I groaned. Our future looked grim. Our throats were already raw and hoarse from yelling; our exit blocked by stone; Ollie pinned against the wall; our torches growing dimmer; and we were hungry and thirsty. Most of all, we were terribly scared.

I gave voice to the thought that lurked uppermost in our minds.

"What if we don't never get out?"

"Don't say that!" Ollie cried. He was in pain besides.

Earl took up where I left off. "What if we die here?"

"Yes, an' what happens when a body dies?" I added, remembering Aunt Cordie's cold, still form, and the many times I had transgressed in my short lifetime.

"I don't wanna die," Ollie said in a low, shaky voice, and I said I didn't either.

"Maybe we'ns could pray," I said suddenly, knowing that in a crisis the average hill folk were apt to become more pious than usual.

We bowed our heads and asked the Lord to help us find our way out of the cave — and we would be good boys forever after. Amen.

Encouraged, Earl figured we might as well try to free Ollie. He braced himself against the side of the corridor with one knee, practically straddling the sides of the cave, and slowly but surely lifted the stone that held Ollie a prisoner.

With a relieved sigh Ollie crawled away. We were still in the heart of the mountain and didn't know if we'd ever be found, but we piled away the blockage stone by stone. One by one our pine knot torches flickered and went out and we found ourselves in darkness so thick it could almost be felt.

Once more we shouted to Chester for help. Again our anguished cries reverberated with a hollow echo through the long, ghostly passage to mingle with the ceaseless water drip of centuries.

Blindly we groped through the blackness, making our way down the tunnel.

Suddenly Earl, who was in the lead, gave a joyous cry. "Look! Ain't that a light up ahead?"

A pinpoint of light! Could it really be the opening to the cave? Keeping our eyes on the tiny speck we scrambled through the dank, mossy corridor and shortly

54

we reached the mouth of the cave.

As we tumbled into broad daylight, exhausted from our cave ordeal and almost blinded by the bright sunlight, we found Chester squatting on a slab of rock, nonchalantly doodling on the ground with a crooked stick.

"Sure took you long," he muttered sullenly.

"Long?" Ollie yelled. "We was lost! Didn't y'all hear us holler?"

"Nope. Nary a sound."

We were quiet.

Our excitement at having discovered what we felt sure was the "Jesse James cave" was dimmed by the fact that we were lost. We might have died in the bowels of the earth, and only by God's grace had we found the right aisle to safety. We thought about it for a long time. Could God have cared enough to have a reason for sparing our lives?

I couldn't help but wonder for what purpose He had saved mine.

6

When I was eleven we moved back to the Kentucky hills, this time settling in a two-roomed house plus kitchen and woodshed which sat on stilts of split logs four feet off the ground. It was located on a semi-island in the middle of Licking River.

A narrow neck of land barely a wagon's width joined us to the mainland. Yet when the river rose during a heavy rain we were forced to ford the stream and climb up the grassy slopes, walk a mile or two, and hop across the swinging bridge that spanned one prong of the river.

We settled back into the lethargic, change-resisting pattern of the hills, plowing our cornfields with a singlebottom plow pulled by a cantankerous old mule. We resumed our diet of corn bread and buttermilk which we got from our other grandparents who lived across the river. Sometimes we were lucky to have salt-cured bacon or squirrel and molasses to enliven our meager meals.

Of course, we hauled our corn to the mill where it was ground into meal, and the sugarcane to the molasses shed where the stalks were fed into a horse-driven contraption which extracted the sweet clear juice for the syrup. This was then boiled in huge vats until it turned a golden brown, "finger-lickin' good."

Earl and I planted, hoed, and harvested the crops mostly by ourselves, for Dad worked elsewhere when he could find a job. He often bragged about us.

"Yup," he'd say, "my boys, they raise the best cane in the county."

He was right — at least, about me. There was nothing I liked better than "raising Cain" as a rebellious young upstart.

I remember the night my crippled uncle Charlie and I decided to throw a scare into Uncle Tom who lived up the hill a piece. Uncle Charlie hobbled on homemade crutches as a result of polio, but he wasn't lazy. How often had I seen him seated on the ground, cross-legged, chopping wood for our school-teacher, Miss Welles, and others.

We regarded Uncle Tom as a coward, and we meant to prove it.

Wading across the river, Uncle Charlie and I fortified ourselves with a supply of rocks and crawled through a field of broom grass until we neared Uncle Tom's shanty.

The tin roof glistened brightly in the moonlight. We heaved up the rocks one at a time and let them clatter noisily on the tin housetop. Then we lay back in the grass and hugged our knees with laughter as we waited for him to "turn tail and run."

Apparently Uncle Tom had lost his sissy streak, for he marched boldly onto the little bare porch and fired his shotgun into the general direction of where we were hiding.

"We'uns better beat it," I said soberly. "He could take a good bead on us and fill us full of buckshot."

We stumbled to our feet and raced down the brier-covered hill — right smack into a barbwire fence, tearing our clothes and flesh with jagged cuts. Uncle Tom had stood up to us and we couldn't awe him any more.

One day while paddling down the river, Uncle Charlie and I found a moonshine still hidden in a clump of wild plum bushes. We remained mum, perhaps because it was the "code of the hills" to be loyal.

During the school term we crossed the swinging bridge and loped up the beaten path to Licking River schoolhouse. We were about two dozen husky mountain pupils in this one-roomed frame school which squatted at one end of the Licking River village. One outhouse served both sexes — at different times, of course. One could tell if it was "busy" by the sign that was hung out: IN USE. The girls came to school in feed-sack dresses and we boys wore ragged knee-patched trousers and faded shirts. We gave Miss Welles a rough time, but her switchings for us boys — some larger than she — never seemed very effective.

At times the schoolhouse also served as a church — whenever the hill folk deemed it necessary to hear a fire-and-brimstone message. Grandpa Miller, looking pious with a Bible under his arm and wearing a clean blue shirt, marched solemnly down the mountainside. Somehow, I was never convinced to change my heathen ways because I saw *no change* in the lives of so-called Christians. Moonshine and tobacco and swearwords were common to sinner and saint alike.

Mom had a quick temper and I a mischievous nature, and the two just didn't mix. I hated the poor food and the poverty, and didn't like living on an island, wading every time I wanted to go some place, I suppose I was independent and stubborn as well, partly because of the grim, passive attitude of the hill folk who were reluctant to change. It exasperated me and I fought back the only way I knew by rebelling against my elders.

Mom did her best to train her "young'uns" right, but I didn't appreciate her fiery temper that accompanied her "raisin'" nor her green willow switches. When I misbehaved I got quickly out of her reach.

One day after another argument with her, I decided to run away. I took out across Licking River and trundled up the mountain to the lonely cabin of an old bachelor friend of the family, who I was sure was born with a sympathetic ear. Sitting before the open fireplace in his log cabin, he listened as I spilled out my problems, and then invited me to stay for the night. The next morning he turned to me and said,

"You orten't to worry your Ma this way, boy, bein' gone all night an' all. Tell you what. We'll fix things an' maybe she'll come around."

He packed up a sackful of raw beets for me to take home and as I ambled up the twisting mountain path the sunlight hammered on the white rocks which gleamed like a liquid wash of light. In the grass clustered the tiny blue harebells and the bold flames of the mountain laurel. But I couldn't keep my mind on the exotic scenery. How would Mom receive me?

She was waiting, eyeing my sack of beets eagerly as

I splashed through the river and came slowly toward the house.

"What you done got in that sack, Paul?" she asked in her usual passive tone of voice.

I held out the beets to her. "Somethin' to eat, Mom. Somethin' besides corn bread and molasses and squirrel for a change."

If I expected another switching for having run away, it didn't come. For Mom must have forgiven me because I'd brought a peace offering.

Yet the constant hopelessness, the losing battle against perpetual poverty and despair began to batter me down. I'd grown into a gangly twelve-year-old, and my spirit cringed when I let myself think about these passive attitudes that resisted change in the hills.

For weeks I'd grown restless and undecided, revolting inwardly at the emptiness of life. The hopeless poverty, the bleak hand-to-mouth existence, the odd brightness in the eyes of the mountain people appalled me. It was as if pain or anxiety turned lights on in their eyes; as if an inner chaos suddenly generated activity in an otherwise inactive body. The "woods" in my life had grown too dark and deep for comfort.

As summer wore into fall my restlessness increased. I could stand it no longer.

Dad and I were in the cornfield when I blurted out my concern to him.

"Look, Dad, I cain't take all this bein' poor and never gettin' nowhere no more. I'd like to go away — back to Clarksville, mebbe — an' be on my own."

Dad spat his tobacco chaw across the corn rows

and shifted his blue gaze to the ground. "What about help, boy? I be needin' you in the fields with the work."

"Earl's still around," I said. "Y'all kin make out."

"You're awful young, Paul. You won't never make it."

"I've done toler'ble good on my own so far," I said with a shrug of my broadening shoulders.

"Well, why don't y'all wait 'til the corn's laid by?" he said finally.

I shook my head stubbornly. "No, Dad. I want to leave now — the sooner the quicker. It's a long piece to walk, you know."

He stared with eyes narrowed against the yellowing horizon for a long time.

"All right, Paul. If that's what you want."

I ambled to the house and began to collect my few belongings: A couple of cat's-eye marbles, odd bits of string, and several items of tattered clothing all went into a brown paper bag, plus a handful of cornbread-and-molasses sandwiches.

With one last lingering glance I turned away from the little house on stilts and struck out across the hills northward toward Ohio.

The air was chill, but the mists were rising, and a long band of rich warm light lay over the sloping spur of Licking River. The mists clung with long white fingers to the jack oak and cottonwoods, and then a light wind scurried through the trees and showered the mist drops down.

I was leaving the hills. Yet somehow I sensed I was striking out for a new beginning, a new life.

7

After a long, exhausting trek, augmented by thumbed rides, I eventually reached Clarksville, Ohio.

Dragging my tired figure up the Hiles' dusty driveway I was delighted to hear Mrs. Hiles' glad cry:

"Well, if it ain't Paul Miller!"

Bill Hiles' black eyebrows bristled faintly as he stuck out a hammy paw.

"Goot to see you, Pee Wee."

"It's good to see you, too," I mumbled wearily, thinking: *it'll be especially good to eat Mrs. Hiles' good cookin' again*. . . .

Later it was decided that I was to work for Samuel LaForge, the Hiles' son-in-law, who lived on a dairy farm some three or four miles north of Clarksville. Sam was a thin, stern man with a sharp temper. He demanded respect and he got it.

Motherly Mrs. LaForge bounced around like a rubber ball. I found it hard to believe that this bulk of kindness had once weighed into the world at a mere pound-and-a-half!

Of course, Junior LaForge, who was my age, should have been ecstatic about my arrival, I assumed; yet somehow he wasn't. We had more fun fighting than anyone I know, including my brother Earl.

The large, two-story brick house not far from the highway had all the home comforts I'd dreamed about

62

but never experienced, and I fit into my new life without effort.

The LaForges, like the Hiles before them, were kind to me. They disciplined me, provided me with good clothes and plenty of food, and sent me to school. Junior and I rode the bus into Clarksville each day.

I helped my share in milking the twenty-five dairy cows every morning and evening. I also drove the horses in fieldwork. Sometimes I rode along on the John Deere tractor, sitting behind Sam who was at the wheel.

Apparently Junior didn't like the attention I got and tried to get even with me now and then. At one time we secretly sparred with pitchforks in the haymow. As I dodged and cowered and lunged, he let the fork fly. It sailed toward me. With a wild cry I jerked aside quickly, and it missed me. Except for one tine which plunged through my light-weight boots and into my toe.

In spite of our differences, Junior and I collaborated on some fun. One project backfired. We'd heard that if you took a crow and slit its tongue, it could be made to talk. In a frenzy of squawking and wing-flapping it submitted to capture.

While Junior held the crow's head, I wielded a sharp, ugly razor blade.

"Steady now!" Junior yelled, and I clamped my lips together and pried the bird's jaws apart.

The tongue had to be slit just right. *Trrrrrt!*

With an enraged screech the crow jerked — and the razor slipped, severing the tongue completely. We had to kill the poor crow after that and give up our talking-bird project.

One day Junior and I decided to play cowboys. Instead of horses we'd ride yearlings, we decided. We raced around the corral, picking out our mounts. I roped mine and sprang on its back. But the calf was in no cooperative mood, and began to rear and buck. I flew off and landed unceremoniously headfirst into the manure pile. That ended my calf-riding venture.

The week's highlight was our Saturday night trip to Morrow. Loading our cream and eggs into the old Model A, we bounced into town. Once there, Junior and I gratefully received our "allowance" to spend on gum and soda pop, besides our fare to the movie. Sam moseyed into the tavern to drink beer and play cards. Mrs. LaForge traded the cream and eggs for the weekly supply of groceries. My greatest regret was that there was only one Saturday in a week!

Just when my life became more meaningful and satisfying with the LaForges, my parents moved back to Clarksville. As usual, the only place available was a filthy, rundown frame shack. The owner had been using it as a chicken coop.

After he shooed out the hens and swept out the nests, we moved in — lock, stock, and junk. We visited the city dump for cast-off furniture and broken-down toys, and life resumed its poverty-riddled, hopeless routine. Dad went back to work in Dayton and commuted home for weekends.

He had insisted I rejoin the family circle. I resisted for a while but in the end Dad had his way and I left the comfortable life at the LaForges' and crowded into the three-roomed dump with my family.

When I was thirteen a bright-eyed little girl named Judy came into my life. The first faint flutterings of puppy love stirred within me, and I was sure that Judy was the "one and only." Perhaps it was the innate longing to leave our continual filth and poverty that prompted me to find an escape from my meager, humdrum existence.

That summer I was offered a job as attendant in a visiting carnival in nearby Wilmington. My job was to set up bottles in a tent which the people paid to knock down. I found a room above the garage belonging to Judy's grandparents and began the exciting life in the noisy, insistent carnival. The buttery smell of fresh popcorn, the faint-sticky-sweet whiffs of cotton candy, the odor of roasting peanuts, the blare of merry-go-round music, the hoarse voices of barkers — everything clamored that this was the life for me.

Since I had completed the eighth grade in school and couldn't afford to go to high school. I begged Dad for permission to travel with the carnival when it pulled up stakes in Wilmington and moved on its itinerary.

But Dad was adamant. "No, Paul. You ain't goin'. What kind of life could them gypsy, restless carnival people give you?"

What kind of life are you giving me? I asked myself bitterly. Nothing but the poverty, the filth, and the hopelessness of being poor. Would I ever escape it?

Then one day a fantastic idea struck me. Why not leave home again? This time I'd go far enough away so I wouldn't have to live under the sagging broken-

65

down roof of my father. I'd grown ashamed of our constant rags, our queer hillbilly drawl. Well, I'd shake off the hill vernacular, and I'd live and talk like other folks.

Several of my cousins had left home at an early age and had made their way in life. Why couldn't I? The thought became a piteous crying inside of me.

When I mentioned it to Dad, he demurred. "But you're too young, Paul. You won't never make it."

"I kin — can — do as good on my own as what you give me!" I flung out bitterly. "And besides, I'll hole up in Dayton with kinfolks 'til I get a job. So I won't really be alone."

After a long, deliberate sigh he nodded his head. "All right, boy. You kin go — whenever you git ready."

Gray, mizzling rain had fallen all day, and everything dripped and splashed and wept. The afternoon fitted my mood like a thick wet glove, and after I had milked the cow, Mom and I got into one of our odious arguments. The time to leave was *now*.

I stalked out of the house without bothering to pick up even one ragged pair of pants, and plodded down the muddy driveway. The half-mile to the highway seemed a million miles away. I didn't really want to leave; but I was sick — sick of the everlasting, immeasurable phantom of poverty that had haunted me all my life. I had to seek escape — escape. . . .

Down the rain-swept highway I dragged my bare feet, hoping some passing motorist would stop to pick me up. But the cars only flung up careless arcs of muddy water as they splattered past, throwing back their grimy reflections on the puddles and blurring my vision as though an artist had rubbed his thumb across the dingy-gray landscape.

I had walked about two or three miles when a late-model car slowed down. One of the two men in the front seat rolled down his window.

"Wanna ride, kid?"

I reached eagerly for the door handle. "Sure do. Hey, this is swell." I settled gratefully into the back-seat.

As the car started it moved faster and faster down the wet highway. I tensed, watching the dismal gray scenery whiz by. Goose bumps budded down my spine and I shivered.

"Ain't — aren't you goin' kinda fast?" I finally blurted.

The two men laughed.

"Look, kid, we'll show you what this crate can do," One of them jerked out harshly.

The car continued to gather speed as it raced down the wet asphalt toward the sharp curve ahead. As it careened around the slippery bend and shot across the railroad tracks, it somersaulted crazily, rolling over two or three times before it crumpled to a stop in front of a telephone pole.

I was stunned from the impact and was only vaguely aware that the two had pulled me from the wreck, dragged me to the railroad tracks, beat me unconscious with a piece of railroad iron, and flung me on the tracks and left. Too dazed and helpless to resist I closed my eyes and let the welcome blackness of oblivion wash over me. . . .

8

I don't know how long I lay on those gleaming rails, but in my half-conscious state I dragged myself to my feet and began to wander aimlessly down the middle of the highway.

When the sheriff pulled up alongside, he drew me inside his car and questioned me. As we drove toward nearby Xenia I told him the whole story: how I was hitchhiking in the rain and how the two men had picked me up and all about the crash shortly after.

In Xenia the doctor examined me and said I would be all right. The sheriff evidently believed my story for he promptly set out on a manhunt. Not too far from the wreck he caught the two men who were hiding along the tracks. Upon further investigation the sheriff learned that they had escaped from the Kentucky state prison. They had stolen the car, and after the accident they had been afraid I would identify them. So they beat me up and left me to die on the tracks, perhaps hoping that my mangled body — after the train came — would be found, and that I might even be blamed for stealing the car!

After resting and regaining my balance, I hit the road once more — appointment: Dayton, where uncles, aunts, and cousins would take me in. One innate thing with hill people was that the welcome mat was always out to one's kinfolk.

I knew I'd have to look for a job to earn my own way as my cousins had done. To make myself look mature I darkened my face with a bit of charcoal to fake "five o'clock shadow" — a lesson I probably learned from Uncle J.H. — and made the rounds to Dayton's factories.

One look at my youngish build and thin, boyish face usually decided the personnel director. And I'd experience the hurt all over again every time I'd march briskly up to the desk to ask for a simple job, only to be told:

"Look, kid, why don't you go home and grow up? Then come back in about five years and maybe we'll have something for you."

These rebuffs angered me and I grew bitter and lonely, and young as I was, I wondered sometimes if life were really worth living.

One day while pounding the pavement again, I decided to try one more place. The personnel manager, to get rid of me, tossed an application blank for me to fill out.

Elated, I found a cousin to help me fill out the form. We threw ourselves onto the ground and leaned against a telephone pole.

As we sat chewing on our pencils, a boy walked up to us and began to pick on us for no apparent reason.

I guess I took after Mom who wasn't afraid to tackle anything. (We sometimes said she'd fight a running sawmill!) Jumping to my feet I placed my hands on my hips and yelled:

"What do you think you're doin'?"

He eyed me shrewdly. "Oh, so you want to get smart, do you, kid?"

Deliberately drawing off my coat and shirt and tossing my hat on top of the bundle, I handed them to my cousin. Without warning I let that kid have it, right on his mouth! I didn't quit until I had really worked him over.

Just about at that time one of his buddies approached and I expected to get a few licks myself.

But some of my hill-cousins started toward us and the fight was off.

As the boys turned to leave, one of them turned back and hollered,

"You *would* pick on a kid with just one hand, wouldn't you?"

It was then I noticed that the boy whom I had beaten up had only one hand. I revolted at my own stupidity and felt miserable for my beastly behavior. I never fought again.

After days of searching I finally landed a job at the Farmer's Fruit Market where I prepared fruits and vegetables to sell and did much of the custodial work.

Even though I'd intended to cut all family ties, I decided to move in with Dad who rented a sleeping room in Dayton where he stayed during the week while working at the foundry. I'd bring home fruits and vegetables from the market which were to be thrown into the garbage at the end of the day. My favorite was overripe bananas.

When the novelty of this job wore off after some months I decided to hitchhike to Columbus, Ohio, to

70

live with Uncle Ernie and Aunt Pearl.

Uncle Ernie reminded me of a bantam rooster by his strutting walk, and I developed a real liking for him. He seemed to take to me and took me along on his job as truck driver for the United Moving and Storage Company. To me, he had reached the apex of society with his responsible job, and I yearned to become a truck driver too. Without pay, I accompanied him on his trips through thirteen states, helping load and unload the furniture van. The work of lugging refrigerators, freezers, stoves, and other heavy pieces up and down flights of stairs wore on me.

One day I was particularly miffed when we moved a preacher's three or four thousand books in large boxes, and I wished I'd never have to move another book. At that time I couldn't understand what preachers needed books for anyway, if they had the Bible. I vowed that a preacher was the *last* thing I'd be!

It was against company rules to pick up hitchhikers, especially women, and we never did. But once while traveling through Texas we passed a shabbily-dressed woman thumbing a ride. We drove rather slowly and after a mile or two, we had to stop at an intersection. To our surprise this same woman jumped on the running board and demanded a ride! She had hopped onto the half-loaded tailgate as we drove by and caught her ride without our knowledge.

Sometimes when I grew too tired and sleepy I'd pile up the padding quilts to make a bed in the van and sleep as the truck rolled down the highway.

I finally found a job at Kresge's five-and-ten in the

toy department assembling and selling toys. By now I had grown into a lanky teenager of seventeen.

After working in the five-and-ten for some time I grew bored. Life just wasn't getting me anywhere, and I wanted to widen my horizons. Being always conscious of money, I'd saved a substantial nest egg of eighty dollars.

One day Earl and I got a zany idea. We decided to travel. Maybe another part of the country would have more to offer than Columbus. Thumbing a ride to Texas, and apart from searching for jobs, we'd see some country — the biggest country ever.

I quit my dime-store job and we packed a few things in a bundle and set out. The first day we almost wore out our thumbs wagging them at cars that rolled past us on the highway.

Disgusted, I stuck out my tongue at the next car that sped past. The man in the car braked sharply, backed up, and really chewed us out, lacing his language with a streak of unprintable words. But at the end of his tirade he opened the car door and told us to hop in.

After days of walking and hitchhiking by turns we reached the last lap to Fort Worth via truck. All that first day we pounded the pavement looking for work, but nothing seemed available to us.

"We'd better find a place to sleep," Earl said with a tired sigh at the end of the day. We found a flophouse at 50¢ a night.

Wearily we undressed and crawled into the sagging bed. Our effort to sleep was punctuated by bites from fellow bed companions who apparently resented our intrusion. Or else they were happy at the thought of fresh blood. It wasn't our first experience with bedbugs but we appreciated it even less because we were so fagged out. The night grew oppressively warm and we opened the windows wide.

Mid the blare and clangor of the noisy streets we heard singing. It sounded good to us and we got dressed for a closer look. As we sauntered across the street we saw a blazing sign: RESCUE MISSION. Missions usually fed a person if you came in, and we walked in hungrily and listened to more gospel singing.

After the evening service we dragged ourselves wearily back to our room and tried to sleep.

The next day we thumbed a ride to Dallas. Perhaps this larger city would have the right jobs for us. But after days of searching we were forced to admit that, large as Texas was, it wasn't looking for us, and we might as well go back home.

Thumbing our way across the country, eating at greasy hamburger joints, and sleeping in cheap hotels, we finally landed in a little town in Missouri. By this time we had run out of money. Night had fallen and we had no place to sleep. Besides, we were dead tired and hungry from our long trip.

"Let's see if we can locate a bed for the night," I said to Earl.

He perked up his ears. "Without money? Are you crazy? Where?"

We stood around and deliberated.

A policeman who noticed our hesitation ambled toward us. "You kids looking for someone? Or do I book you for vagrancy?"

Quickly we told him that were were hunting for a place to sleep but that we had no money.

"We'll fix you a free bunk at the city jail," he told us, and we followed him gratefully to a small 8 x 10 ft. cell in the town's hoosegow.

We entered the dingy cell and tumbled into the bunk for a much-needed rest. We had just drifted off to sleep when we were awakened by a terrible noise. Someone stomped around and yelled at the top of his lungs. In the dim light of an overhanging bulb we saw a sloppy, dissipated drunk staggering into the jail.

"You boys better git outta my bed, an' you'd better git out quick!" he growled. Weaving his way toward us, he chased us out of his cell. Mayberry-fashion, he locked himself in, crawled into one of the bunks, and in seconds he was snoring like the proverbial elephant! Earl and I slept the rest of the night on a big table in the hall.

The next morning we turned our footsteps back to Columbus.

I became confused and unhappy about life and began to nurture romantic illusions when I met Aunt Pearl's sister Shirley. She was twice my age and two times widowed when her husbands had passed away. Perhaps she represented the class and security which I lacked, and before long we decided to be married.

When we applied for a marriage license at the courthouse the clerk behind the desk roared with laughter.

"Why don't you grow up, kid?" he choked out between guffaws. "She's old enough to be your mother!"

I wanted to jump over the desk and punch his nose, but I restrained myself and we left.

We decided to go to Kentucky to be married, for the laws in regard to age weren't as stringent.

She returned to her home in Northern Ohio to dispose of her house and furniture and I moved in with my sister Evalee and her husband Dick in the meantime.

Saturday night I paged restlessly through the newspaper in my loneliness. My eyes caught the popular "wishing well." This is a numerical puzzle with a coded message designed to spell out the reader's fortune. In sheer boredom I worked out the code, using my key number which was 4. The message I decoded said simply: *Go to church Sunday.*

Go to church? I'd seen enough of hypocrite hillbilly religion to last a lifetime. I threw down the paper in disgust and went to bed.

Sunday would be just another interminable day dragging with bitter loneliness. As usual, I spent the day at the movies. After I'd sat through the double feature it was evening and I decided I might as well go home.

When I hopped on the crowded trolley, there was only one seat left, which was beside a pert, sweet-faced little woman, Mrs. Bonar.

After a few moments she turned to me. "Son, why don't you come to church with me tonight?"

I hooted with laughter. "Ma'am," I said, "the roof would fall in if I set foot inside a church house. I've never made it a habit to go to church an' I'm not aimin' to start now!" I lapsed into hillbilly vernacular in my derision.

The trolley clanged down the street and I saw my corner coming up ahead. I guess I had grown uneasy, sitting beside this radiant, dynamic little woman and I wanted to get off.

As I reached up to pull the buzzer cord she said again, "Son, I sure wish you'd go with me tonight."

It was as though someone grabbed my shoulder and held me in my seat. My hand froze.

Stunned, I replied simply, "OK, I'll go."

We walked into the First Church of the Nazarene when we stepped off the trolley. People greeted us warmly. Rev. Simmons, the pastor, was conducting a series of special meetings. The congregation seemed to possess something I longed to have, as though their lives radiated purpose and meaning. If only I could be a part of it!

I've forgotten the pastor's text after these many years. I only know that the Holy Spirit wooed me that night with the words: "Come unto me, all ye that labour and are heavy laden, and I will give you rest. Take my yoke upon you, and learn of me; for I am meek and lowly in heart: and ye shall find rest unto your souls" (Mt. 11:28, 29).

Rest — from a storm-tossed life . . . from loneliness and despair. This is what I wanted! I was in the proper mood to listen and with an inner ear I heard Jesus offer His pardon and peace — free for the taking.

At the invitation hymn, I found myself walking toward the altar. "Just as I am. I *come!*" I come, Lord — poor white trash as I am — I come with my bad temper, my stubbornness, my self-will, my bullheaded desire to change my own life.

Kneeling there in that simple white frame church, I found forgiveness for my sins.

When love came in, hatred and self went out. My life has never been the same since. I had come out of the "woods" of frustration and despair and into the sunlight of God's grace!

The next day I called Shirley and told her that our marriage was off.

What was the next step for me? I didn't know. But from now on I had a Guide and I would walk wherever He led.

First Church of the Nazarene, Columbus, Ohio, where Paul became a Christian in 1949.

BOOK TWO *"Promises"*

1

The gnawing emptiness of my life had been filled when I knelt at the altar of the Nazarene church. And now another hunger nagged at me: to rise above the poverty and apathy to which I had been born. Yet how could I — without opportunities? Wherein lay the answer?

My brother-in-law had served in the United States Navy and his gripping stories of sailing the seas challenged my dry existence. Some inner urge compelled me to consider enlisting in the Navy, for I felt that anything would be better than what I had. Perhaps it might be the stepping-stone I needed to extricate myself from my bonds. Too, I loved my country and this was one means of showing my appreciation. Maybe God even had a niche for me to fill here.

I went to the naval recruiting station and asked for enlistment papers. To my surprise I easily passed both physical and written tests, and within days I was on my way to boot camp in San Diego, California, along with several other raw recruits. Here was another promise I had to keep in my life.

Arriving at the training center we were pushed through lines continually, it seemed. There were the medics; the forms to be filled out; the chow lines; and there were also the barbers. Like sheep before the shearers we waited in line for our crew cuts. My hair had always been unruly and it was almost a relief to get it lopped off.

I remember one recruit who had a crop of thick, wavy black hair. As he slumped into the barber's chair I overhead the barber ask:

"You wanna keep this gorgeous hair, son?"

"Sho' do," drawled the obviously conceited young man.

Without a word the barber snipped off the handsome waves and tossed them expertly into the bewildered fellow's hand. "Here y'are, son. Next!"

After tests and inoculations by the dozens, we were issued our complete Navy outfits: shoes too large and baggy pants — the whole works — including a canvas seabag which could hold *everything* — provided we knew how to fold *everything* according to specifications.

In short, the Navy provided me with some of my basic needs, which included clean clothes, fresh linens, good food, dental care — and most of all, discipline — and there was plenty of that. Up at five, we scrambled into our clothes. Our beds had to be made so tight a coin could bounce when the inspecting officer tested them, and our shoes shined until our bell-bottoms almost mirrored themselves.

One way of obtaining discipline was by making the whole company suffer for one person's mistake. Of course, we watched ourselves because we didn't want our buddies' wrath upon us.

I'll never forget big rawboned "Skunkie" who refused to take a bath. His body odor had gotten the whole company into trouble and we chafed under it. To discipline him, several of the men grabbed him one night when he came in, stripped him naked, and hauled him into the shower, then scrubbed him with a hard-bristled GI brush and granular GI soap until he was raw. Skunkie never missed taking his bath after that.

One of my best friends was Billy Brown. To a young Christian such as I, Billy seemed heaven-sent. We studied our Bibles in company with each other, and when allowed liberty, we went together.

One free weekend Billy and I drove to San Diego where we visited Balboa Zoo Park, and other places of interest. During our rambling along the streets we met a girl whose face and figure would have wowed any male.

She winked at us and motioned toward a small picture-taking shop.

"I've never seen a handsomer pair of sailors than the two of you," she said in a sultry voice. "How's about getting your pictures took here?"

Billy and I looked at each other. "Handsome sailors"? That was us, all right! It would be nice to send pictures to folks back home, and we entered her shop.

While she set up her scenery and equipment she made other suggestions.

"Look, you guys," she said coyly, "for an additional fee I'll kiss you while we're taking your pictures. OK?"

Billy and I glanced at each other again. Without a word we swung around and marched out, sans pictures.

In my Bible study I came frequently upon verses which stressed believer's baptism, and that to follow Christ meant to be obedient to Him. When I asked

81

the chaplain about it he gladly baptized me by immersion upon the confession of my faith in Jesus Christ as the Son of God and my personal Savior.

After I finished boot training I was assigned to Pearl Harbor. En route I stood on the bow (or fantail) of the destroyer and watched the dark green water surge and pound against the ship as it shashed through the sea. Overhead sea gulls wheeled and arrowed through the blue skies. The rise and fall of the ship didn't bother me at first, and I laughed as others doubled up over the handrail and heaved their insides out, their faces becoming a bilious green, and their bodies weak and spent. My turn came later.

Before we reached Pearl Harbor the Korean conflict exploded into a full-scale war, and the captain received orders to move full speed ahead to Korea. The rudder split due to the full throttle and the radar mechanism fell off. We limped into Pearl Harbor where the ship was dry-docked for several weeks before it could go on to Korea. Lucky for me that this became my destination, for I was stationed at the IFDDG (Inactive Floating Dry Docks Group), and assigned to the maintenance of ships and floating dry docks which were no longer being used. Our job was to go from craft to craft, chipping paint and preparing decks and bulkheads for paint applications of red lead and navy gray. The work was a boring, never-ending job.

I spent all my spare time in Honolulu. The city is extraordinarily beautiful. The public parks and gardens are profuse with exotic tropical flora; the museum noted for collections of zoological, ethnographic, and historical materials related to the

Hawaiian Islands; the Waikiki beach for its rolling waves and white-beached sands.

I sought churches, however, as being of real importance to my life, and attended both the Waikiki and the Kaimiki Nazarene churches. The local people were wonderful. I especially learned to love Mr. and Mrs. Willard Bolling and their two small children, Wilma June and Tommy, who attended the Waikiki church. We became fast friends and I spent most of my liberty in their home. Willard Bolling gave me a real boost and became genuinely concerned that I prepare for a vocation after I got out of the Navy.

From Pearl Harbor I was transferred to the Kileauea Military Camp of the Big Island of Hawaii. This camp lies almost in the shadow of Mauna Loa, an active volcano and near the Kileauea Crater, also potentially volcanic.

I spent liberty at Hilo where I again sought a church. Here I met the Baublitzes who were missionary builders with the Assembly of God Church.

Once while I was on an island excursion with the Baublitz boys we wandered around the hills where we discovered underground lava tubes — like tunnels or caves. Of course, these differed widely from our "Jesse James" cave in the Appalachians. In exploring these caves we came upon fragments of human bones along the ledges, and as a souvenir I picked up an almost perfect set of teeth. We learned later that these lava tubes served as burial places in the past.

I knew the Baublitz family lived "by faith" although often there was little to eat. Their Thanksgiving fare would be very meager, I realized, and on an impulse I asked the officer in charge of food supplies at the base if I could take some food to these good people.

"Sure, Paul," he said kindly. "Take what you need. But remember, I didn't see you do it!"

The Baublitzes had a Chevy carryall and the two boys and I backed it up to the storage house and loaded it with frozen turkey with all the trimmings and hauled it to their home in Hilo. They invited me to eat Thanksgiving dinner with them. Mrs. Baublitz was an excellent cook, and I could have learned much from her that would have helped me in my next experience.

The camp's only baker had been transferred and I was assigned to take his place. Any experience in Mom's primitive kitchen was of no help here.

I'll never forget my first culinary masterpiece. Carefully I followed directions for mixing up a chocolate cake, pouring the thick, creamy batter into huge cake pans. It seemed a bit crusty on top and a mite doughy on the inside when I took the pans from the ovens. I cut the cake into squares, however, and proudly placed the platters on the service tables and returned to the bakery.

Suddenly my senior officer stood before me with fire in his eyes and a piece of my chocolate cake in his hand. He shoved it under my nose.

"Miller, just what do you call this?" he bellowed.

"That's cake, sir," I said a bit shakily.

"Cake, eh?" he roared, and added some unprintable expletives. Then he told me to dump the whole mess into the garbage.

84

Needless to say, I served ice cream for dessert that night.

One Sunday night after spending the weekend with the Baublitz family, I drove back to camp with the Baublitz boys, for I was to be on duty around midnight.

Just as we entered the bakeshop the whole sky seemed to explode with a brilliant orange-red color and a deafening rumble shook the earth.

"Kileauea Crater!" Link Baublitz yelled, and we jumped back into the car and raced toward the blazing inferno. Spewing white-hot lava hundreds of feet into the air, the volcano gave a spectacular performance. We paused fascinated to watch. If this is what hell is like, I thought, I'm glad by the grace of God that I'm not going there!

Rev. and Mrs. Rueben Welch came to Hilo as Nazarene missionaries to organize a church and construct a church building. One of the California churches had sent a Studebaker pickup truck with a canvased canopy in which to haul Sunday school kids. We worked with new and used lumber, and obtained doors and windows from an old hospital. The great day arrived when the church was finished and we conducted our first worship service. I am a charter member there. Working on this simple church and helping with the services and hauling kids to Sunday school in the pickup truck, I recalled the promise which I'd expressed that long-ago day when I stepped on the nail back in the Kentucky hills and went to Miss Madge Carter for help. "Some day I'm going to be a preacher. . . ."

To enter the ministry and serve the Lord actively

Paul D. Miller,
U.S. Navy, 1949-
1952.

Nazarene Mission Church, Kauailani and Nohea streets, Hilo, Hawaii, which Paul helped to build during his free time while in the Navy.

became a challenge. Yet it was so completely out of the question that I practically thrust it from my mind. I knew that it would take years of education to prepare myself for such a gigantic task. And how dared I — a product of poverty and an example of "poor white trash" who hadn't the means to go to high school, much less college — think of such a thing? Frankly, this responsibility looked bleak.

During a thirty-day leave in Ohio with my family I became all the more determined to make something of my life and leave the apathy and degradation behind me. After a brief stint at Seattle, I received orders to return to San Diego where I was placed on the *U.S.S. Curtiss*, a converted seaplane tender. Again we were ordered to Pearl Harbor and the dry docks for overhaul, where I was overjoyed to meet my old friends on the tropical islands.

I had served nearly four years in the United States Navy but had never participated in active combat, and now I was almost ready to be discharged.

Shortly before my discharge in August of 1953, the educational officer who had become my good friend, asked me why I didn't finish high school.

"Finish? Why, sir, I never had the chance to start!" I said.

He looked at me somewhat in surprise, and told me that during my few remaining months in the Navy I could prepare myself to enter college by taking the G.E.D. (General Educational Development) tests, administered by the Armed Forces Institute. If I passed them I would be eligible for college.

College! My heart raced crazily. Never in my

wildest dreams had I considered going to college. Was this why I had felt the urge to go into the service? Was it leading me somewhere?

I couldn't make college, I told myself. But I took the tests and waited impatiently for the results.

Then one day I received the overwhelming news that I had passed all the tests and was eligible to attend the college of my choice. The words almost stunned me. God, in His divine wisdom and guidance, had permitted me to take my first step out of a life of deprivation to prepare me for His service. I'll walk, I decided, wherever He leads me.

In my gratefulness I claimed Paul's promise in Philippians 4:13 as my life's motto:

"I can do all things through Christ which strengtheneth me."

2

The following September in 1953 I enrolled as a freshman at Olivet Nazarene College in Kankakee, Illinois. After I paid my tuition I used what little money I had left to buy clothes from the Goodwill store.

With something like awe I gazed at the cluster of college buildings, hardly daring to believe it was true and I was really in college.

For a while I stumbled around in a sort of daze, but this didn't last long. College students are expected to study and I was no exception. Still, I thrilled at the ivy-covered halls, the winding, shrubberied drives, and the throng of students milling about the campus. I was one of them!

The Ad building, built of imposing limestone, loomed at the college entrance. My quarters were in Chapman Hall for men, which sat across from Williams Hall, the girls' dorm.

At first I sold Wear-Ever pots and pans from door to door to earn extra money. Later I took a job as baker at the college cafeteria (my skill had noticeably improved, I hoped, since the chocolate cake episode in the Navy) which left little time for other things, besides studying.

Olivet, being a Christian liberal arts college, had its principles founded upon God's Word, aimed at helping students to grow spiritually. I literally sopped up Bible knowledge, for I never lost sight of my goal of becoming a minister of the gospel.

For some time I had observed an attractive girl at the dishwasher and I went around and asked some questions. I found out her name was Marilyn Zinn; she was a plumber's daughter; and she hailed from Michigan. Marilyn was 5' 6" tall and graceful, with delicately molded, slightly oriental features, brown eyes, and rich dark hair that fell over her forehead like a crow's wing. Somehow whenever I'd see her, my pulse raced crazily. I yearned to ask her for a date. But that took nerve.

One day I saw her scraping a plate into the garbage disposal. I clawed together the necessary courage and slipped up behind her.

"How about a date tonight, Marilyn?" I said with feigned casualness.

Startled, she whirled around and the plate she was scraping shattered onto the floor.

Needless to say, she accepted the date.

Marilyn's mother had prayed that she would find a Christian for a mate and from the very beginning we hit it off well. Since I had little money to spare we double-dated with another couple and played Monopoly; attended school functions, or went picnicking. But we managed to see each other frequently, and often read our Bibles and prayed together.

Once we planned a birthday date in Rock Creek Park and wound up in lover's lane where I told her I loved her. She admitted she felt the same about me.

I tried to express my love in different ways. Once when she had a slight cold I sent her a dozen red roses. She cried over them and almost scolded me for my extravagance. But she was so excited she took twelve snapshots of them!

Being a product of the hills I possessed a very practical streak. Therefore, instead of an engagement ring I gave Marilyn a set of Rogers 1847 silver plate silverware in June of 1954. Appropriately, it was named Proposal.

Having met her family I decided it was time for her to meet mine. I tried to warn her of the poverty in which they lived, but she wasn't totally prepared when we drove to Ohio that summer.

I had sent some of my mustering-out pay to my parents with the stipulation that they get something "really nice," for Mom had always made do with almost nothing. To my dismay they used the money to help buy an abandoned, ramshackle schoolhouse which had to be propped up with poles on one side to keep it from toppling over.

As we pulled into the yard, weeds and broken limbs choked the place. A bedraggled field of sunflowers flanked one side of the house. A bit of this and a wisp of that, a few scraps of rag, and some battered tin cans littered the sagging porch. A broken chair and a rusty hoe leaned against the front stoop.

Grunting pigs wallowed from under the house as I helped Marilyn out of the car.

Mom, her dress wrinkled and damp with sweat, rushed out and gave Marilyn a hearty hug.

"So nice to meet Paul's girl," she said warmly, and opened the door to the house. The school building had been partitioned off into three separate rooms with cardboard for walls. The kitchen looked as though a huge eggbeater had whipped its contents into a heterogeneous mixture. The black range was covered with a sooty water kettle and a huge paint pail of wet mash for the hogs. Backless chairs were strewn with old newspapers, dirty tea towels, and clipping-crammed shoe boxes. Mom shoved the mess effortlessly to the floor and invited the bewildered Marilyn to "set."

For our first meal Mom had fixed fried woodchuck with biscuits and gravy. I didn't blame Marilyn for gagging. Although the meat was dark and succulent they ate ravenously. Someone waved a tree limb back and forth over the table to shoo away the flies.

Marilyn stared goggle-eyed at the cardboard rooms; she cringed at the sight of the shotgun beside Mom's bed where she was to sleep (when Mom would hear a noise at night she'd shoot first and ask questions later); and a plumber's daughter that Marilyn was, she almost rebelled at going to the outdoor "john" which sat some distance away from the house. Walking through the dense, dark night with coyotes howling in the distance appalled her. No wonder she was upset!

But as a valiant, sincere Christian, Marilyn Zinn warmed to my family and accepted them with Christ's love. I loved her all the more for it.

We decided to be married on August 14 of that summer. Several days before our wedding the finance company repossessed my little car and I had to catch a ride to St. Louis, Michigan, for our wedding. I hadn't told my bride of this, but it did pose some honeymoon problems.

Our wedding, which took place in the Nazarene Church, was small: a few college friends and members of her family were all that were present. On the guest list were Art Salisbury and his wife Norma (Art served as my best man), Art's wife, Norma, served as matron of honor; my roommate, Bob Collins, and Dick Fry ushered while Harriet Bircher sang the solos. My family, of course, couldn't afford to come. They did send us a bedspread as a wedding gift, however. Marilyn wore the traditional white gown and veil belonging to her older sister, and to me she looked more beautiful than ever. For a fleeting moment it occurred to me that since the church is the bride of Christ, it should be as spotless and lovely as Marilyn was that day.

We drove to Bud Lake at Harrison, Michigan, in a car we borrowed from Don and Jeannette Nelson for a brief two-day honeymoon. After a short stopover at her parents' home, we returned to Kankakee where we set up housekeeping in a tiny house trailer. It was filthy when I first found it and I'd spent hours cleaning and painting so I could offer my bride something better than what I'd known during my life.

Our college friends turned out for a bang-up charivari shortly after. Our supper dishes were still on the table when they burst into our door. The menfolk boldly grabbed me while the women took Marilyn, and dressed us in long white underwear. Then they drove us into the country in separate cars.

The sun had long left its smoldering fire above the distant hills and night, with a smothering blackness, had fallen. As we turned in at the cemetery gate, I was catapulted from the car and before I could catch my breath, it revved its motor and was gone. I realized with a shudder that Marilyn was some place in the ghostly gloom of the graveyard too. But where?

There we were — two spooky figures in our white underwear, flitting and stumbling among the cold, granite tombstones, trying to find each other in the impenetrable blackness. Before long we were in each other's arms. But we were unsure of the right road back to town.

Laughing hilariously and holding hands we began a lonely walk back to our little home. Dogs barked, crickets chirped, and we heard the hoot of an owl. Otherwise the cold black night seemed motionless.

In our rambling we came upon several men fixing a waterline who told us how to get back to town. Later, when our friends returned to pick us up they asked the men if they had seen us.

"Yeh," one of them mumbled, "just a few minutes ago we seen two guys in white tuxedoes walk by." Our friends nearly exploded with laughter.

Arriving back at our trailer house we found all the labels ripped from our supply of canned goods, and rice strewn everywhere. Weeks later we discovered rice grains deeply imbedded in the pockets of our clothes hanging in the tiny closet. Unfortunately the mice had found them too.

We both settled down to our studies. I worked wherever I could and Marilyn also held down a job. Life flowed smoothly in our cozy love nest — or so I thought.

When I returned home one night after work I found my wife sprawled on the bed, crying her heart out.

"What's wrong, honey?" I asked gently, stroking her thick dark hair.

She choked out between sobs. "Oh, Paul — I know you did the best you could — and I can put up with the cramped quarters. But that — that *thing!*" She pointed derisively to the covered "night vessel" which served as our "indoor toilet" facilities. To empty it we waited modestly until after dark, for its contents had to be carried a block down the street to be dumped.

Again the "plumber's daughter" found it difficult to adjust to primitive living conditions — things that weren't new to me.

We decided to spend our first Christmas in Ohio with my family. Marilyn had skimped and saved and gone on a shopping spree. She bought presents for each member of my family and wrapped them in gaily-colored holiday paper, tied with curled ribbon. I knew how much this would mean, for Christmastime to a family of poor country folks like mine hardly ever included many gifts. She also spent extra time baking cookies to take along.

Previously we'd bought a '37 Plymouth and this time Marilyn was better prepared for the trip to Ohio. But I saw the heartrending glance in her eyes as she caught sight of the scrawny little pine which my brother David had cut from the hillside and decorated bravely with colored paper chains and other home-made doodads. It did something to us to watch Mom,

Dad, and the kids unwrap their gifts.

It seemed that we could never overcome our financial straits, and once while driving home from a trip with only fifty cents between us, we heard a rumbling, grinding noise from the innards of our Plymouth.

I glanced at Marilyn and shook my head. "Honey, I'm afraid the transmission's going."

"Is that bad?"

"*Expensively* bad," I said. "We can't afford a piece of baling wire, much less a breakdown. What are we going to do?"

The grinding grew louder and I expected the car to shudder to a stop at any moment.

Marilyn leaned against my shoulder and whispered softly, "We can pray, Paul. Remember, *God can fix that transmission!*"

Dear, wonderful Marilyn! While I drove, she prayed, begging God to "fix" that transmission, because, as she reminded Him, we had no money to have it repaired.

God heard that prayer, for the rumbling noise began to grow less, and by the time we reached Kankakee it had stopped altogether.

Marilyn and I worked out a secret code between us. The word "ditto" meant "I love you," and we used it to "sign off" telephone conversations with each other, or whenever we had to part and others were present. I know I was heartened to hear her say, "ditto" when she'd call me from her job and I was worried about her. Somehow I knew that things were all right with her, after she repeated our code word.

96

Because of our financial difficulties I worked for the Gould Battery Company at night and struggled through school during the day. Marilyn was working with the General Foods Corporation and we barely skimmed along.

When Marilyn became pregnant with our first child and school was out, I took on a full-time job with the Bata Shoe Company. New responsibilities thrust all kinds of wrinkles into my life. Just when it happened, I don't know, but I began to take my eyes off the Lord and looked to myself for our needs. Perhaps it was also partly because I'd become disillusioned with Christianity when a certain Christian had failed to live up to his moral obligations. At least, this is what I told myself. It was while I was working for Bourbonnais Cleaners that our baby girl, whom we named Kay Lani, made her arrival on January 12, 1957. Bitterness had gradually seeped into my soul and I became almost obsessed with the idea of taking care of my wife and baby. I quit the cleaners and started working for the Bata Shoe Company again. But I neglected to read the Bible and we stopped going to church altogether. Our spiritual life had grown very dim.

Perhaps this was why my temper began to rule me again and I got mad at my boss at Bata's and after an argument one Monday morning I walked out, leaving my door keys on the counter. In a few days I found a job with the Smith-Alsop Paint Company.

We had moved into a three-roomed house in Bradley, Illinois. Mr. and Mrs. Morris Tooper, the owners, have become our lifelong friends. In my

97

desperation to earn a living I had tried many jobs. I became afraid, for I didn't want to be ignorant and rap out the rest of my life in poverty.

On January 3, 1959, our second daughter, Kassandra, was born, and we moved to an upstairs apartment on the other side of the city.

I grew more restless and dissatisfied, even though I had worked my way up as assistant manager in two jobs, I felt there was no future for me with either of these two firms, and I became angry with the whole world.

Without consulting Marilyn I'd bought a house on Hickory Street on contract. It looked like a hovel when I first saw it, for it was filthy and very run down. It had possibilities, however, and I worked all hours of the night, cleaning and fixing it up. When we moved in, it was cold enough to light the furnace. The heat brought out the horrible stench of urine which had dribbled in and permeated the ductwork. The odor was unbearable and Marilyn began to weep uncontrollably. Finally, in desperation I took her and the two little girls to her parents' home in Michigan.

I was forced to sell all our furniture and appliances at a considerable loss, but nothing mattered now. We were done with Kankakee and its territory and we would move some place else — any place — where we could be happy.

We decided to move to Colorado. This young, vigorous state seemed to beckon us. We stashed our few earthly possessions in the car and a U-Haul trailer. After staying a week with the Toopers, we left Illinois on Easter Sunday, March 1959, and set our faces westward.

When we arrived in Loveland we had $200 in cash, no job, and no place to live. And our promise to the Lord all but forgotten. . . .

3

We moved into a motel apartment and I went job hunting. In a few days I landed a job with the Loveland Trailer Factory. My work was setting nails and puttying nail holes. I hated this job so much that I decided even digging ditches would be more exciting. I gave it up, and after working for a shoe store for a few weeks I looked for still another job. My restlessness was still there.

Since I had worked in a paint store back in Illinois I felt somehow drawn to the Vorreiter Paint Company.

The boss was on the phone when I walked into the store, and while I waited for him to finish his conversation I wandered around the store, studying the brands of paint on the shelves.

Then we talked, and after we had conversed for a while he made a rather startling request.

"Why don't you and your family come to our house tonight, Miller? I like to look over a prospective family before I make up my mind."

With some trepidation I took Marilyn and the two little girls to see the Vorreiters. We must have made a passing grade for he hired me as a salesman right away.

After working for some time, Mr. Vorreiter approached me with a suggestion. "Wouldn't it be good

100

for business if you and your family went to church?"

Of course, as a paint salesman I wanted to become better known. My wife and I talked it over.

"Which church shall it be?" she asked, folding the freshly washed diapers which always seemed to be there in stacks.

I winked at her. "Let's try them all. Then we'll take our pick."

We attended several churches, searching for one that would answer our needs. They all seemed to lack the warmth we groped for.

Then we tried the First Methodist Church. The people, warm and friendly, and full of faults as a piece of cheese has holes, accepted us as we were. Rev. Ken Smith, and Robert Spears, the associate pastor, together with Paul Holdeman, all welcomed us heartily and showed a tremendous concern for us which we sensed immediately. The more we attended that church, the more our spiritual reserve broke down, and we soon found ourselves a part of this fellowship of believers.

Due to a business slump, Mr. Vorreiter was forced to let me go. However, he helped me to get a job as manager of the Stone Furniture Company, which was owned by Ray and Dixie Rider, formerly of Clay Center, Kansas.

The real impact of the church's love hit us in 1960 on Layman's Sunday when I was asked to speak on "How to Be a Christian in Business." Reluctantly I promised. This made me dig deep into my Bible and thrust me onto my knees; but apparently the Lord used my message to speak to the people.

Person after person pumped my hand after the service ended. "Paul, you ought to be in the ministry," they told me. "You're in the wrong business."

It reminded me of the promise I had made to the missionary in Lee City years ago: "Some day I'm going to be a preacher." And also it reechoed the challenge I had received while working with the missionaries in Hawaii.

At work the next day God told me almost the same thing as the people the day before. *What about your promise, Paul Miller?* Was I any good at keeping promises? After all, I had served my country well; and I'd made my promise to take care of my wife when I repeated the wedding vows. It wasn't exactly a Damascus-road-type of experience when another Paul so many years before had cried out: "Lord, what wilt thou have me to do?" And yet mine too was an encounter with the Holy Spirit.

Is this it, Lord? Do You really need me? . . . *Yes, Paul, I need you. . . .* But I'm weak and poor and full of self-will and faults. . . . *You can do all things — overcome — in My strength, Paul. I'll walk ahead . . . you walk after Me . . . follow Me.*

I finally broke down. "Yes, Lord, if You'll open the doors, I'll walk through them," I cried. Oh, the peace that flowed through me as I yielded my will to Him was like coming out again into sunlight after being shut up in a dark room!

One weekend some time later we drove to Scandia, Kansas, to visit some old college friends, Ford and Carol Miller. Ford was pastoring the Methodist church there and when I discussed my call with him he arranged for me to meet Dr. Mancil Bell, the Methodist district superintendent.

Dr. Bell suggested that by correspondence I take the introductory studies for a license to preach, and upon completion of the course I would be granted the license to preach. Then he'd find a church for me. Of course, I would need to finish my college eventually.

In the meantime I worked by day and studied by night. When I had finished the course I waited a church assignment from Dr. Bell. We moved out of our house and into a motel apartment belonging to our friends, the Robert Mitchells. The waiting was hard.

Time dragged interminably until the call came. We were to take the charge at Broughton, Kansas, on June 5, 1961.

We had gone to Broughton briefly one weekend while visiting Ford and Carol on a hunch that perhaps this might some day be our charge. Broughton was a tiny hamlet sitting quietly beside a dusty Kansas wheat field. The white frame church, nine or ten dwellings, an auto repair shop, a quaint post office, and an elevator comprised the town. Two railroad tracks angled along one end almost like an afterthought — the Rock Island past the church, and the Union Pacific crawled near the parsonage. As we entered the church I walked impulsively to the pulpit and stood behind it. A strange feeling swept over me. Would I stand behind this sacred desk some day and preach?

When the call came that verified our contemplation, we couldn't keep the news to ourselves. Soon everyone in our church at Loveland knew about it.

"Broughton's really just a wide place in the road," I told our friends offhandedly. "A white frame church and a couple of cottonwoods, plus a handful of houses. And the town's only electric light pole is right in front of the parsonage."

"Yeah. Think of the parsonage. I'll bet it's two rooms and a path!" someone joshed.

"And tornadoes." Another warning. "Leaving Colorado's lovely mountains for the flat, dry plains of Kansas with its rattlesnakes and tornadoes — you must be crazy!"

But underneath all the good-natured ribbing our friends stood behind us with their prayers and best wishes.

With mixed feelings Marilyn and I began to pack our belongings into a U-Haul trailer which we would pull behind our '53 Buick.

One thing bothered us: after paying off our debts we were down to our last few dollars — not enough to pay the gas for our move to Broughton. We had to trust the Lord to supply our needs somehow. The trailer wasn't packed right and we unloaded everything and repacked. Again, things didn't want to fit in and we were forced to take everything out and reload for the third time before we could finally be on our way.

As I berated myself mentally for having wasted all that valuable time because I hadn't packed it right the first time, I saw Mrs. Robert Mitchell, a member of the Loveland Methodist Women's Society of Christian Service, amble over. She handed me a package.

104

"With love and best wishes from the WSCS," she said casually.

I took the gift and thanked her. It was a copy of Catherine Marshall's *Mr. Jones, Meet the Master*, a book I'd always wanted. As I began to page through it, my eyes widened with surprise. For spaced all through the book lay crisp green one dollar bills — fifty of them! The Lord had kept us long enough in Colorado to provide for our move to Kansas.

At Wray, Kansas, we stopped to eat our lunch, realizing we'd need to dip into our much-needed financial hoard which had to stretch until our first paycheck. But we went into a cafe and were seated at a table waiting to give our order when some friends from Loveland walked in. Of course, they came to our table — and when they left they paid our bill.

We stayed with Ford and Carol Miller at Scandia the first night. They supplied us with abundant help and encouragement and sent us on our way the next morning.

The June day had grown unseasonably warm as our Buick grunted down the road, pulling the loaded trailer behind it. Suddenly — *sss-boom!* — one tire blew out, and the car shuddered to a stop.

The sun beat some 100 degrees hot as I clanged with tools and a jack, and my fresh slacks grew sweat-stained and grimy.

Marilyn threw one glance at me and snorted, "If you ask me, you don't look like my idea of a new preacher!"

"Oh, the congregation will take us for tramps and feed us — I hope!" I cracked back.

Broughton drowsed lazily in the late afternoon sun

as we rattled down its single unpaved street. The white frame church clearly dominated the town, while the few substantial houses in various stages of disrepair were scattered comfortably down the street. Side roads wandered aimlessly off the main street now and then and disappeared into the wheat field.

As we pulled up before the two-story parsonage we sesnsed a flutter of activity. Women, smudged with paint and dirt and wearing prints or faded jeans, were wielding brushes and mops as we walked through the front door.

Later we learned that eleven-year-old Julie Chapman had waited impatiently at the parsonage all afternoon, eager for her first glimpse of "the new preachers." Her mother, Mrs. Leo Chapman, had been called home; however, the excited Julie had been given permission to stay. When our tired Buick grunted to a stop, Julie caught sight of us. As Marilyn and our daughters wore their dark hair straight and cut with bangs, and having faintly oriental features, Julie gasped. Then she rushed to the phone and called up her mother.

"Oh, Mom, the preachers are here," she babbled breathlessly,"and I think they're Chinese!"

While the "plumber's daughter" scooted up the stairs to seek out a bathroom (she found one upstairs and a half-bath down), I was smothered with handshakes and introductions.

As I inspected the downstairs rooms I pulled open a half-closed closet door.

There I noticed a pair of long white legs and my gaze traveled up to a face crowned with a shower of pale blond hair. While I batted my eyes, the woman shrilled,

"It's only me — Cathy Haney!" And she grinned at me from her latex-spattered face while she continued to slap paint on the closet walls. Cathy remains our dear friend to this day.

After we had unpacked our trailer and crept into bed that night. I lay tense and tired, almost too weary to sleep. A hot breeze hung limply over the window-sill without stirring. Thoughts, impressions, and plans tumbled and whirled through my mind. I had told the Lord I would follow Him, for I had "promises to keep." So He had led us here. But what did I know about conducting a church service? And what made me think I could preach to a congregation of 125 souls?

My musing was rudely interrupted by a sudden heavy roar that screamed through the blackness.

A tornado — on our first night in Kansas! My Colorado friends knew what they were talking about.

I jumped out of bed, grabbed a flashlight, and yelled at Marilyn:

"Get the kids — and follow me out to the storm cellar!"

I grabbed Kay Lani and dashed down the stairs, with Marilyn carrying Kassie. Playing the flashlight across the uncertain steps and through the kitchen I led out to the back porch. Where was the lashing wind, the fury in the trees which I'd always asso-ciated with a tornado? A brilliant light was flashing across the backyard, and as my fingers gripped the handle to the cellar door it dawned on me. This was no tornado — it was the night freight as it rumbled

107

and screamed on its late run across the plains!

The first Sunday of my new charge dawned bright and hot. Marilyn's hands shook as she cooked breakfast. She was sick, she said, and begged me to let her stay at home. Finally I relented.

"Paul, how *can* you be so calm this morning?" she demanded. "Aren't you in the least bit nervous?"

Nervous? Of course, I was nervous. But God starched my backbone so I could stand calmly behind the pulpit that morning and announce my text: "The Meaning of Life." Not only my congregation of rural folk, but I too, sensed the Holy Spirit's presence in that little country church that morning. I was finding answers for myself as well.

We had a wonderful time that day, climaxing the fellowship in the church basement at noon with all the fried chicken and potato salad we could eat, during which someone read an anonymous poem written by someone with a literary quirk as a welcome for the occasion:

WELCOME

We welcome you with much good will,
As each new duty you fulfill.
The Broughton folks have gathered here
To get acquainted and spread good cheer.
As you take up each new deed,
We are certain you'll succeed!
So as you come to this new station,
We know you have a reputation
Of being folks with courage to press on,
Just like Peter, Paul, and John.
Patience and love o'er all outpoured —

Leading lost souls to the Lord —
Helping those who go astray
To trust in Jesus every day.
So we look forward without fear
That we will have a prosperous year!

During that first week I was asked to conduct my first funeral service. I have never in all the years of my ministry refused to offer comfort to the bereaved when asked to conduct similar services. Color, race, or creed has never stopped me.

That fall I enrolled as a student at Kansas State University at Manhattan, commuting a distance of thirty-five miles each way, in order to continue my college education. The Loveland, Colorado, church played a large part in financing my college that first year with generous gifts at different times — both privately and from the church as a whole.

In 1963 the pastor of the Hayes Methodist Church passed away and I was asked to take on that charge as well. Serving two churches while attending college kept me busy. But I was happier than I had ever been in my life. These two congregations of honest, warmhearted Christians had embraced us with all the love in their hearts. I threw myself wholeheartedly into my work.

4

A preacher's life seldom leaves a private corner untouched. For the parsonage — and the inhabitants thereof — totally belong to the church and congregation, as we soon discovered.

While we pastored the Broughton, Hayes, and Ebenezer churches in Clay County we became very close to them. They were not only parishioners; they became also our friends.

I recall the countless times that I have laughed with my people, cried with my people, and have suffered and prayed with them. I have felt the pangs of death when they were passing through the valley of the shadow. Weddings, funerals, and just plain everyday experiences of life have enriched and endeared these people to our hearts. For such is the life of a man of the cloth.

After we arrived at the Broughton parsonage on June 5, 1961, our lives took on a different hue from what they had held heretofore. I was often called "the preacher" although I was mostly referred to as "Reverend Paul." Our children received the customary moniker of "P.K's" (preacher's kids).

Kay Lani, a pert four-year-old, and Kassandra, an endearing two, soon navigated their way around the small village, and before long they had made friends with everyone.

"Just remember to stay between the two railroad tracks," Marilyn told them firmly, and they did

At first the two little girls ventured no further than to the telephone office where they loved to watch Viola Mosburg's practiced fingers manipulate the switchboard. Sometimes they crawled onto her lap, and occasionally she let them "listen in" on the telephone conversations.

In time they braved the longer trek to the post office and soon were regular callers there. The fact that the postmistress, Mrs. Joe Haney, sold candy became an added attraction, although I strictly forbade the girls to ask for any.

Of course, Mrs. Haney's heart melted when she'd see those two pairs of soft brown eyes peering wistfully at the candy and bubblegun in the cabinet. It was only natural when Kay Lani entered the first grade that she would stop at the post office with her carefully hoarded pennies and buy her own bubblegum on her way to school. Nancy Bauer took on the role of big sister and always walked with her.

Mrs. Haney grew somewhat concerned over all that bubblegum and one day she decided to question her little customer.

"Kay Lani, does the teacher allow you to chew gum in school?"

Kay Lani shifted her glance to the ceiling, rolled her big brown eyes, and replied hesitantly: "Well . . . not out loud!"

Yes, life in a parsonage can never be termed dull.

One day when I was on a drive in the country I decided to visit a parishioner. As I drove onto the farmyard I noticed tall, gangly Wayne beating his dog with a rooster. Feathers flew as the dog yapped.

Wayne paused in his unorthodox act and eyed me curiously as I got out of the car.

"Hi, Reveren' Paul."

"What in the world are you doing?" I asked in bewilderment.

He grinned lopsidedly and shook his head. "Well, this dog eats chickens, preacher. And I read some place that if you beat a dog with the very thing he's been pesterin', he'll quit. So I'm hopin' he'll leave chickens alone after this."

But you've had to kill the chicken to prove it. I thought to myself.

Wayne shrugged nonchalantly and tossed the chicken aside. It rolled over onto its feet, croaked, and staggered away, still quite alive. We both stared dumbfounded!

I had a penchant for trading cars, and in the four years that I served the Broughton church I owned a Chrysler, two Volkswagen bugs, and a Volkswagen Microbus. It was while driving one of the "bugs" that my family took to wearing dark sunglasses while out riding.

One of my parishioners had met us on our way to town one day and remarked candidly to a friend:

"The Millers all wore sunglasses, and I'll declare — in that VW they looked like a nest of owls!"

The spring following our arrival the Broughton congregation voted to paint the parsonage. No one complained at first of Marilyn's color choice which was charcoal gray with white trim, although secretly it

112

bothered some of the more conservative members. The "painting bee" with the men doing the painting and the women providing a basket dinner at noon made short work of the renovation job. Eventually they all "forgave" us, not only the charcoal color, but also the fuschia-colored front door!

I was certainly no Jerome Hines when it came to singing. In fact, I hardly knew how to tote a tune in a bushel basket. We were trying to drum up Sunday school and church attendance and I promised the Broughton church that I would sing a solo if there were 150 people at church on any Sunday. To my surprise the Hayes congregation was invited to worship with Broughton one Sunday. The count was made and the total climbed over 150. I kept my promise and got up before the crowded church to sing. I somehow hacked my way painfully through several verses of "There Is a Balm in Gilead." Later, someone remarked that with that "bomb in Broughton," it would be safer from now on to aim for 150 if I promised *not* to sing!

One summer a couple of our young folks, Colleen Fowles and Russell Terry, had become engaged and made plans to be married in the Ebenezer church. I was to perform the ceremony. The wedding rehearsal took place the night before at seven-thirty, and in my busyness I forgot that the wedding itself was to be held at seven the following evening. We were living in the Clay Center parsonage at the time which served both the Ebenezer and Hayes churches, an eleven-mile drive to Ebenezer. Marilyn, who was to sing a solo, looked radiant in her modish black dress and lovely corsage. We were in the parsonage taking pictures when I glanced at my watch. It said seven-fifteen. Suddenly it hit me.

"Marilyn . . ." I almost shouted. "That wedding was to start at seven, not at seven-thirty!"

We jumped into the Chrysler and took out like a shot. I don't like to confess to breaking the speed law, but I'm sure we did, trying to reach the church as soon as possible.

In the meantime the wedding party and guests were waiting anxiously at the church. What could have happened to the preacher, and why was he late? As an ambulance screamed past the church they were certain we must have met with an accident! The members of the wedding party grew increasingly alarmed.

As our car braked to a grinding stop before the church shortly after, we hastily offered explanations and apologies, and the wedding ceremony began. Marilyn was almost too shaken to sing, but she put her heart into it and the beautiful service was completed.

I remember another wedding for Marsha Siebold and Arnold Pittenger which was held in the Hayes church. Congenial Rosie ("Ironsides") Evans was to be the soloist, and she was on the program to sing just before the vows were repeated. She stood up to sing as the couple and I took our places before the altar. But in my pastorly concern and excitement I failed to notice her standing there with her mouth already open, ready to sing, and I began to read the vows. After the ceremony, the organist immediately modulated into the recessional and the couple walked

Paul D. Miller's first charge, Broughton Methodist Church, Broughton, Kansas, 1961-1965.

"Reverend Paul" standing beside the bulletin board of the Broughton Methodist Church.

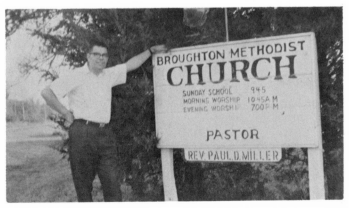

out. Poor Rosie never got to sing her solo!

Before Vincie was born, the Broughton WSCS had planned a surprise cradle shower for Marilyn. Mrs. Leo Chapman had promised to stop by the parsonage for Marilyn, but she was late. Marilyn paced up and down, growing more upset by the minute.

"What's keeping her?" she fumed, stepping in front of the window for the dozenth time. "You know how prompt and dependable Irene is. It's not like her to be late."

When Irene Chapman finally arrived, Marilyn hurried out to the car. I called out, "Ditto, Marilyn," and she smiled faintly and repeated our code. I could see the tenseness written in her face but knew she would be all right when they reached the church.

On the way to the church Irene seemed so full of chatter that the car practically crawled down the road, much to Marilyn's chagrin. Of course, they arrived late and Marilyn's disgust was obvious. Her disgust changed to dismay, then to delight as she caught sight of the many practical baby gifts the women had brought. (Perhaps it reminded her of the first shower she had ever attended as a preacher's wife. She had been told only that it was to be a "shower" — and so she brought a baby's gift — only to learn it was a bridal shower!)

These times of laughter were also intermingled with the deeper things of the spirit. Easter time meant the annual sunrise service. On a hill above the schoolhouse someone had erected a cross, and here the community gathered in the pearly pink dawn to remember the

The noted Catalpa Cross in what is now the Countryside United Methodist Church, Clay County, Kansas.

death and resurrection of our Lord and Savior. One Easter I decided to do something different. While strolling through the nearby woods among the wild crab apple, now a pink and white cascade of fragrance, I looked up for a moment to the high, cauliflower clouds. Then I looked down and saw a clump of catalpas, eaten to the core by ants. On an impulse I cut two of the trees down and fashioned a crude cross — a cross that exactly matched my measurements. Taking it to the Broughton church with the ant-eaten branches plainly visible, I preached a message that Easter on "The Enemies of the Cross." That cross still stands in the church, which later became the Countryside United Methodist Church — a grim reminder of things which hinder a Christian's testimony, and yet

117

vibrant with the glory of the resurrection.

In October of 1963 the Broughton church held a revival with Rev. Oscar Matthews as the evangelist. Cottage prayer meetings had preceded the meetings, but at first it seemed that the people were cold and unresponsive to the message, hindering the work of the Holy Spirit. But on that last night God's love broke through and there were twelve decisions for Christ.

Death, the grim reaper, was no respecter of persons, and the average Christian family calls upon the minister for comfort when the end is near. I shall never forget the young father who died, leaving a wife and two small sons. I had come to be with the valiant woman as her husband gasped his last. She stood there, swept up in an overwhelming sense of lostness, as she realized that his long days of suffering were over and his spirit had flown as it had left his ravaged body behind. I felt my inadequacy to help her through her grief. And yet, even in this, God had called me to serve my people. It was one of the hardest aspects of my ministry.

I also remember the man injured in an automobile accident, lying paralyzed and in a coma for two long, agonizing years. Again I felt a sense of helplessness to comfort this family as they tried to understand why.

Mrs. Helen Sewell, a retired schoolteacher, was a member of the Hayes church at the time I served the congregation. Although she was retired from active teaching, she had undertaken to tutor Lori, a little retarded girl. Helen kept me posted on Lori's progress as the little girl slowly learned to read.

When Helen became gravely ill she called for me. "I'm going to die and I'm ready to meet my Savior, Reverend Paul," she said with deep assurance. Then she gave instructions for her funeral. "My only regret is that I can no longer teach Lori," she added. "I hope someone will be found to take my place." Her voice faltered and broke. My prayers were not for Helen Sewell, but for someone available to teach Lori.

One day while a student at K-State, I was called out of class to answer the plone. It was Marilyn. She told me of a man who lay dying in a Concordia hospital and that his family requested I come immediately.

I jumped into my car and drove to the hospital as fast as I could, to find the man gasping almost his final breath. The family was sure it was only a matter of time. I sat down at his bedside and talked to him of Jesus Christ.

"The Bible says that Jesus came 'to seek and to save that which was lost.' He also says, 'Him that cometh to me I will in no wise cast out.' In Isaiah we read, 'Seek ye the Lord while he may be found, call ye upon him while he is near.' Sam, do you believe this? And would you like to accept Him now?"

His voice was very weak but it throbbed with certainty. "Yes. I want to accept Jesus into my life — now."

He asked for baptism then, and with a bit of water I baptized him upon the confession of his faith in Jesus Christ. To everyone's amazement Sam recovered and was able to return to his home several weeks later.

One year I was asked to participate in the Union

119

Good Friday service at Clay Center. Shortly before the service I was called out to see a woman who was in desperate need of help. I called my Presbyterian pastor-friend, Bruce Henderson, and asked him to pinch-hit for me in the service. He was willing.

When I arrived at the woman's home I found her stretched out on the divan sobbing brokenly. I sensed she was in a mental turmoil, for she had lost all will to live. Nothing seemed to reach her.

I sat beside her and talked at great length, reading the Bible and praying. She seemed completely beside herself. Finally I asked her if she would do me a favor and seek psychiatric help. At first she would hear nothing of it, but after much persuasion she agreed. I helped set up an appointment for psychiatric treatment which she kept. She returned after a short period of resident treatment, a healthy, happy, and well-adjusted person.

And so my part in God's plan became as unshakable as the rolling Kansas hills, flowing like wine-colored sacrament into the deep hollows surrounding my people. Whether I understood how or not, I knew that God was using me.

5

Commuting thirty-five miles to and from Kansas State University at Manhattan twice a day; pastoring two Methodist churches; caring for my family's needs — grew to be for me a heavy load. Twice I was forced to withdraw from college: once because we found ourselves in a financial bind and I couldn't afford to continue; the other due to illness in the family — which is a story in itself.

I suppose I hold some sort of record for the length of time it took me to finish college. Twelve years after I enrolled at Olivet College, at Kankakee, Illinois, I donned my cap and gown at Kansas State University, Manhattan, Kansas, and paced rhythmically through the long line to receive my diploma. Miles and Paula Henry had accompanied us on graduation day and we celebrated with a dinner at Holiday Inn later.

I am grateful to God and to my family and friends for making this event a reality in my life, for it was a real achievement since I had never graduated from *anything* before!

However, I must confess that college wasn't easy for me, particularly during my senior year because I was burdened with the many pressures, difficult decisions, and emotional strains of closing the Broughton church and preparing to move to Clay Center. (It wasn't until 1970 that I finished my theological training and was ordained, but I had at least reached the first educational milestone in my life.)

Next door to us lived Viola Mosburg. She was familiarly known as "Central," the community's telephone operator. To our girls she was like a grandmother, and to us she was ever a dear friend. When Marilyn was expecting our third child, Viola's motherly concern proved a real boon in those difficult days.

Viola had come over to stay with the girls when I rushed Marilyn to St. Mary's Hospital in Manhattan when the baby's arrival was imminent. While she lay in the labor room I strolled down the quiet corridors to the nursery windows and watched the newborn infants. They all seemed so small.

"Just you wait until my son comes along," I told those squalling red-faced infants, "and he'll really show you up."

Our son, Vincent Paul, made his grand entry prematurely shortly after, on August 19, 1962. He weighed in at five pounds and 9 1/2 ounces. I thought my buttons would burst.

He seemed fine, and the fact that he was small and unable to suck didn't unduly alarm us, since he was a month premature. We knew that for several days he had to be fed with a tube to his stomach.

When Marilyn was ready to leave the hospital, Vincie had to remain until he reached a reasonable weight level. Our friends, Wayne and Dorothy Carlson offered to help me bring Marilyn home. Our girls listened wide-eyed as Marilyn told them about their little baby brother whom they would have home some day soon. Then the doctor called us on the phone.

"I'm sorry to alarm you, but your baby has a blood problem. He'll need a complete transfusion," he told us. "We'll have to start it immediately."

Stunned, we looked at each other. We had heard of the RH negative blood factor, and that if the baby's blood differs from the mother's the child faces almost certain death unless the blood is changed.

Just after the call, one of our church ladies stopped and said the women were gathering for special prayer that afternoon. It seemed that there was always someone praying for us when we needed it most.

Wayne and I left immediately for Manhattan and we stayed until the intravenous transfusion was completed. It took six hours, and we were relieved when it was over. I sat moodily in the waiting room, my heart pounding with trepidation. To have a son who might some day follow in his father's footsteps — and who might never leave the hospital alive . . . I shuddered.

Sister Ann-Loretta rustled up beside me. "We've done all we can, so don't you worry," she said brightly. "The rest is up to God." With her calm conviction I believed it too.

Although Vincie remained weak for some time, he held his own in the days that followed. I was amazed at Sister Ann-Loretta's devoted attention to him. She stayed up during the night when she was off duty just to watch and feed him. When she asked me once as a minister of the gospel to pray for her, I somehow felt led to tell her that she should pray for *me* instead. I'd never witnessed such intense devotion before.

Shortly before Vincie's birth we had purchased our

first new car, a Volkswagen. During the period of the baby's critical condition when I rushed to Manhattan to the hospital one afternoon, a bird dog loped across the highway in the front of my car and in spite of all I could do, I hit the dog and he was killed on impact.

I got out of the car and looked at the crumpled mass of bloody fur, and surveyed the damage to the front bumper and fender of the car.

A woman hurried out of the farmhouse across the road. I could see she was terribly upset. She picked up the mangled, broken dog in her arms and began to cry. Then she berated me sharply for my carelessness.

"This dog meant a great deal to me. And now you've killed him," she added bitterly.

"I'm sorry," I said in a bleak tone of voice. "I know I drove fast. Maybe too fast. But I was in such a rush to get to the hospital. . . ." I found myself telling her all about Vincie's struggle for life.

Suddenly the hard lines faded from her face and it grew soft with concern and sympathy.

"Forgive me," she said apologetically. "I didn't realize. What's the life of a dog compared to that of a child?"

Vincie improved slowly but steadily in the days that followed, and after ten days we were happy to bring him home. He grew round and rosy, without any sign of the trouble that had plagued him at birth.

Little did we know when our third daughter and fourth child Krassina was born that we would again be driven into an agony of spirit. Dr. Heasty had felt it was best to start Marilyn's labor. But after hours of fruitless contractions she was sent home to wait.

However, by Sunday evening she was in such misery that we called Dr. Heasty who said to bring her back the thirty-five miles to the hospital immediately.

After a tedious labor Marilyn gave birth to Krassina on May 18, 1964. We were relieved that it was over at last. Somehow we just weren't too worried at the attitude of the doctors and Sisters, although we sensed that all was not as it should be. But Marilyn was tired and I was concerned only that she was comfortable, and in a hurry to return to my church work.

Dr. Heasty somehow seemed to put off telling us about the trouble until the next day. I was at a meeting at the Hayes church when Marilyn called the Homer Rundles who lived nextdoor to the church. They came and told me of Marilyn's call and that there was something wrong with the baby.

When I sped back to the hospital I found Marilyn almost in a state of shock. The doctor had finally told her there were several things wrong with our Krassina.

"She was born without an *anus*," he had told her frankly. "And there are several growths on her ear lobes."

At the moment this was all he said, although doctors know that when there is one deformity, there are often several.

Marilyn's parents came from Michigan to Broughton to help take care of our other youngsters. When we told them of Krassina's problems they refused to believe it, even when Sister Ann-Loretta held the baby up for them to see.

125

"Why, we've raised ten children, and everyone's as healthy as a horse," Dad Zinn said emphatically.

But being people of tremendous faith, they upheld Krassina earnestly in prayer, believing she would be helped in an operation to correct the absence of a rectal opening.

Dr. Olney had performed surgery on Vincie's hernia in the previous March and we had great faith in him as a surgeon.

He consented to operate on Krassina, although he admitted there was only a fifty-fifty chance of its being a success. But we had felt God's leading so definitely through the prayers of His children that we never doubted for a moment we had made the right decision in asking a local physician instead of a specialist to perform the delicate operation.

Even before surgery, Krassina had been placed in a private room, and Sister Ann-Loretta supervised the special nursing care. We could see her only if we donned sterile gowns and masks, and then just briefly.

When she was wheeled into surgery we waited anxiously for the outcome. Sister Ann-Loretta waited with us.

"Now don't you worry," she said cheerfully. "I've got a bunch of aged nuns who can't do anything anymore but pray. They're in the chapel on their knees right now!"

Several hours later Dr. Olney came out of the operating room and told us Krassina had come through the surgery and she would be all right, but she would need a great deal of special care.

Before we took her home, Dr. Crane, the pediatrician, took us aside. He told us they had discovered her "horseshoe kidneys" — when the two kidneys are fused in horseshoe fashion and function as one. This was a problem which could not be corrected.

It wasn't until later that we learned Krassina had still another abnormality: she had a curvature of the spine. The doctors had known all along but hadn't wanted to worry us. They felt we had enough to bear at the moment. From the time she was a year-and-a-half old until now, Krassina has had periodic checkups at the Kansas Crippled Children's clinic in Salina.

During this trying ordeal the Broughton and Hayes congregations showered us with loving attention, food, and financial aid. Rushing back and forth to the hospital added to my other burdens and we sensed their prayers in a special way for we were strangely buoyed up. Had it not been for this, I might have broken under the strain.

We were forced to admit again that God's promise to us held true: "I will never leave thee, nor forsake thee," and that we could do "all things" because He strengthened us, according to our life's motto.

We were to rely upon it all too soon again.

6

Broughton lay sleepily situated in the midst of a rich agricultural district in the northeastern part of Kansas, almost in the lap of the verdant Republican River Valley. During heavy rains the river overflowed its banks and flooded the fertile farmlands.

In surveying the area, government engineers reasoned that a dam and reservoir built along the valley floor would control the runoff from 3,620 square miles downstream.

The Milford Dam was to be located on the Republican River about ten miles above the confluence of the Republican and Smoky Hill rivers, which form the Kansas River farther along. The dam would provide complete protection to 6,400 acres of farmland along the Republican River below the dam, and together with Tuttle Creek on the Big Blue River, and other existing and authorized reservoirs, would effect a high degree of flood control on the main stem of the Kansas River.

First authorized in 1938, the Milford project was reauthorized in 1953, as a unit of the system of reservoirs of the Kansas River Basin.

With dismay the Broughton congregation learned that the little town was to be leveled in order to become a part of the reservoir.

Now rumors buzzed thick and fast via Viola's

telephone lines, and Mrs. Joe Haney's post office.

"They say that the town will be under deeper'n the light pole."

"They say the elevator's even gonna be under."

"They say Al's garage won't even leave a grease smudge where it's set all these years."

They say. They say. People sitting on the flat top of the post-office stove perked with gossip.

It was time we sifted facts and learned where we stood. Yes, it was true. Broughton as a town was destined to a watery grave. Had it been *on the other side* of the Union Pacific tracks, it would have been safe. The houses, the post office, the elevator, and the garage — *plus* the church — were to be moved to make room for the reservoir. Not only that. Many of the fine surrounding farms were to become part of the reservoir and dam.

The whole shaking-up and tearing-apart was a traumatic experience for the people of the area, especially to my older parishioners. Seeing their thriving farms, built with tender hands and sweat, uprooted and flooded with muddy river water made the people angry. And more than that — to see the church, hub of Broughton's spiritual and social activity — disappear from the face of the earth — well, where was justice?

In spite of the wild protests and the scalding tears the town with its community was destined to go. The government had spoken. I was driven to my knees again and again in the difficult months that followed, because people asked me why this had to be. And I could give them no easy answer. It was so hard for them to become resigned.

In the spring of 1964 negotiations with the engineers about the sale of the church property were begun. The appraiser came, looked over the church and parsonage, jotted a few cold figures on a piece of paper, and left. Some time later we received word from the board of engineers that the congregation was to receive $27,500 for the church property.

We were up in arms. The amount offered for the church property itself was within reason. Yet, what I couldn't condone was the utter disregard for the sentiment, the roots that were being forcibly torn up, the hopes and dreams of years, shattered. And the bastion of spiritual retreat — the church — dispensed with like a trinket over a shop counter.

I was dissatisfied with the engineers' cold-blooded handling of the situation and I tried to get them to change their minds and offer us a larger sum. They practically ignored my letters. In desperation I appealed directly to Lyndon B. Johnson, who was then President of the United States, and told him exactly how we felt. I even enclosed a snapshot of the Broughton Methodist Church.

Then I wrote to the office of the Chief of Engineers and protested the puny remuneration we had been offered. He fired back a reply:

"The district engineer at Kansas City, Missouri, here informed me that on July 2, 1964, negotiations were initiated with the Board of Trustees of the church for the purchase of the church property. As a result of these negotiations, I am informed also that the Board of Trustees executed an offer to sell the church property to the United States for $27,500. Although this offer exceeds our appraised value of the church property, it will be accepted on behalf of the United States. Payment to the church in the amount of the offer will be accomplished by a representative of the district engineers. . . ."

The district engineer was very angry when he came to see us later. As we sat in his official car, discussing the matter, he whirled around and pointed a direct finger at me.

"You have no right to write to the President of the United States about this!" he stormed.

I didn't flinch. "I have *every right*," I said quietly, "when it comes to dealing with intangibles such as the heartstrings that have been snarled in these ruthless negotiations!"

Angrily he retorted, "Don't you know I can get your job for this?"

Could he? Would I be forced to give up preaching the gospel because of the stand I had taken for my people? I didn't doubt God, and I refused to be intimidated.

Letters flew back and forth, and when I'd go to Broughton's tiny two-roomed post office for more heartbreaking mail, Postmistress Haney always had an encouraging word to offer.

"You'll win," she said. "I know you're concerned for us, for you've got God on your side."

Shortly after, we received the following word from the Lieutenant General's office in Washington, D.C.:

"This will acknowledge receipt of your letter, addressed to the President, considering the acquisition of the Methodist church, Broughton, Kansas, in connection with the construction of the Milford Dam and Reservoir project. Since the corps of engineers is responsible for the construction of the Milford project and the acquisition of the land for the project, the President has referred your letter to me for consideration and reply."

The appraiser returned like a whipped pup.

As I replied to the Lieutenant General, I said:

"The appraisers and the negotiators are looking at our situation from the dollar and cents point of view. There is much more to be considered: the functional value, spiritual, moral, and social, to mention a few things; also, we did not have the property up for sale. We have lost — and are losing — several of our active members because of their land being acquired for the Milford project. We have the challenge before us to minister to those who will remain and we hope to meet this challenge. We need your thoughtful consideration."

Not long afterward, negotiators offered the sum of $38,500 for the church building, parsonage, and land. We knew this was the final price. We had no choice and we were forced to accept.

We gathered at the church to decide what to do next. Should we move the church building and relocate? Or should we disband and join other Methodist churches in the area? The district superintendent said the decision was ours.

We approached the Bethany Evangelical United Brethren congregation which lay outside the reservoir area about uniting with us and becoming a part of our congregation, but they weren't ready to do this.

132

Alone, we couldn't carry on.

The idea of what to do was batted pro and con, but in the end the Broughton Methodist group voted 36 to 25 to disband.

The day for the auction of the church property in April of 1965 dawned cloudy and chill. My parishioners huddled in groups, every bid for the church and parsonage like a knife-thrust in their backs. Then it was over. The EUB congregation had bought the 48-year-old church house; a Clay Center family purchased the parsonage. Both would be moved away from their original foundations forever.

Still another question arose. How should we dispense with the money we had acquired for the church property, since we had voted down the suggestion to relocate? We investigated various projects that needed help. But we were agreed that the money should be used for missionary purposes.

When we called a meeting and the church decided how to dispense with the funds, it was voted to use the whole $38,500 for the Kansas Area Methodist Foundation for Missions. The principal was never to be used, but the interest on the money was to be channeled into the operation of the following five mission projects:

— The Ethel Homfeldt work in Africa.
— The Henderson Settlement in Kentucky.
— The Bob Connerly work in Mexico.
— India pastor's support in Pakistan.
— One fifth to be used by the foundation.

The entire $38,500 was to be turned over to the Kansas Area Methodist Foundation in 1965 at the annual conference in Dodge City.

It wasn't easy to try to soothe the troubled souls of the people who had been uprooted by the Milford dam project, but it became my job to point out God's hand in all things and to help strengthen their faith. With true Midwest stamina most of them bounced back and have adjusted to their loss.

With the Broughton church closed, I was left with only the Hayes church. Since the Ebenezer congregation was without a minister I was asked to take their charge as well, and to continue in the Hayes church. In June 1965, we moved to Clay Center into the Ebenezer parsonage. From here I served both churches.

The last letter has long been delivered through the Broughton Post Office, and the last plug is removed from the telephone switchboard. Now the once proud town is a bed for dried weeds tumbling gracefully in the Kansas wind.

7

The community youth carved a special place in my heart, and much of my pastoral life has been centered around their needs and activities. Remembering what a dearth there had been in my own poverty-stricken boyhood, I resolved to help my teenagers to a more meaningful, abundant life.

Kurt LaPlant, a short, stocky redhead with a spatter of freckles over his round face, was about fourteen when our paths first crossed. He lived in one of Broughton's residences and we soon became horseshoe buddies. The clink of iron upon iron as our horseshoes bit the dust became a ringing sound almost every afternoon. Sometimes we grew so absorbed in our games that I forgot about Marilyn's tastily prepared meals which grew cold on the stove while she waited for me to come and eat. Kurt came from a large family and he apparently treasured the attention and friendship I offered him.

It was while I was pastoring the Ebenezer and Hayes churches that Kurt, at eighteen, went into the army. He stopped by the parsonage one evening to tell us good-bye, and added that he was to be sent to Vietnam.

Disturbed at his somewhat flippant attitude, I asked him what he was going to do there.

"Kill people," he said with a short laugh.

I talked to him seriously about his relationship to Jesus Christ and we prayed together, but I wasn't altogether sure where he stood spiritually. His free and easy manner continued to bother me during the time that he spent overseas.

Then one day I received a letter from him, and my fears calmed. Among other things, here is what he wrote:

"Dear Reverend Paul —

I can only bring peace of mind to myself once a day, but it's every day, and that's when I take out my *Upper Room* and my Bible and read the daily Scriptures. This comforts me very, very much when I am alone in my bunker and wondering what the next day will bring. . . . I went to church services Sunday and the battalion has gotten a new chaplain. He's a very nice person. I only hope I can get to know this chaplain like we knew our other chaplain. There is a lot of news but it's all about fighting and dying in Vietnam and I don't want to talk about that. It kind of depresses me to talk about what is going on over here. So I'll cut this a little short and let you go. I'll write again when I get the chance. May God bless you all. Your buddy, Kurt"

Kurt had finally faced life in the right perspective, and I thanked God for it. We didn't hear from him again.

When we received the grim news in 1968 that Kurt was among American casualties in battle with the Vietcong I had the conviction that all was well with him at last.

I was asked to speak at his memorial service held in the old Broughton church which had been moved to its new location and now was called the Countryside United Methodist Church. The catalpa cross still stood sure and firm as a silent reminder of the cross of Jesus Christ. Lights had been wired inside the cross, and their glow was a symbol of the never-failing light of the gospel.

In remembering Kurt, I knew that he had finally reached his haven through that eternal Light!

When we came to Broughton in 1961, all the young people from the ages of twelve to twenty were lumped into a single MYF (Methodist Youth Fellowship). I decided to divide the group, putting the junior hi bracket into a Junior MYF and the high schoolers in a Senior MYF.

The local youth sponsor and his wife were strongly opposed at first. "It will never work," the man told me bluntly. "Young folks all ought to stick together. They got along fine together before you came."

He seemed quite disturbed that I had dared to change the status quo. One day when I had gone to the church to be alone and pray about the matter, he came striding toward me, walking along the tracks that skirted the main street.

"It'll never work," he maintained, but I assured him I meant to try.

I invited both groups to church for Bible study and round table discussions. At the senior hi youth meetings we often stayed up until midnight talking about young people's problems, trying to arrive at the answers they were seeking.

We had gone out for overnight camp-outs now and then, roughing it out in the open and going to Leo's Shack, which was an experience in itself.

One day the young folks begged me to take them on a real camp-out.

"Let's take food, cots — everything we need,'" they said, and so we planned a two-week trip to Palmer Lake in Colorado at Matt's Camp. I'd traded my VW off on a VW Microbus and we loaded it down with much equipment and luggage (not to mention the twelve young people who had signed up for the camp). We also took a Chevy and a pickup which took what we couldn't load. The Leo Chapmans and Dora Laflin went along as sponsors. The VW fairly groaned under the weight and hung low on its axle.

We were forced to jog along at 35 mph down the highway, much to the speed-geared teenagers' disgust.

On one of our sight-seeing trips we got in a race with a Continental Trailways bus. The kids hung out of the windows and back door, challenging the bus driver to pass us. We outran him coming down every hill and it was impossible for him to pass us going uphill. In spite of our load, we beat him to Palmer Lake!

Once we arrived at the camp and unloaded, the kids forgot about their discomfort and really enjoyed themselves. We took turns doing kitchen duty, and hiked out to the woods for our devotions.

The boys, like typical American teenagers, decided to play a joke on the girls one night. But being good boys, they asked my permission first. I consented. A giant moosehead hung on the wall of the dining hall which the boys removed just before taps. They lugged it to the girls' cabin and lifted it up to the

138

high windows.

I was in the dining room at the time but I heard the girls' screams when they caught sight of the antlered head near the windows. Moments later I heard the girls' sponsor, Dora Lou's footsteps pounding up the hard path as she yelled breathlessly:

"Reverend Paul . . . Reverend Paul. . . ."

Trying to keep my face straight I asked casually, "Yes, Dora Lou? What is it?"

"It's those boys — " and she babbled almost incoherently about the moosehead trick and how it had frightened the girls "half to death."

Inwardly I almost exploded with laughter but I kept a poker face and managed to look perturbed.

"I'll go and talk to them right away, so don't worry about a thing," I said and stepped down the dark, shadow-and-moonlight dappled path that led to the boys' cabin.

Speaking loudly enough so she could hear, I began to "chew them out" for their niggardly deed, all the while almost choking with suppressed laughter. The boys pretended to growl at my feigned tongue-lashing. After Dora Lou and the girls were out of earshot we laughed until we almost split.

One night we decided to make pizza pie. Some of the kids worked up the dough and then began to toss it around in a regular dough fight. Some of it missed the hands which were to catch it and landed on the floor several times. We ate it anyway and it tasted great.

Boys somehow enjoy getting a rise out of the girls, and so our male campers decided to challenge the girls to a mountain hike. Those girls posssessed spunk and were determined to show the boys how to climb a mountain. Of course, we sponsors — Leo and Irene Chapman, Dora Lou, and I — were forced to go along. I made it about halfway up where I stretched out to rest. But I watched the rest push, pull, and drag themselves up by sheer force. The boys wouldn't be outdone, after they saw the girls' determined spark; and by the time the kids returned to the foot of the mountain it was the *boys* who threw themselves exhausted on the ground!

My young people's interest in spiritual things grew, and before long their number doubled in size. The dissenting youth sponsor came to me and apologized.

"You were right and I was wrong," he said. "Those two groups do work better apart." We became the best of friends after that.

Then there was young Ernie, cocksure and arrogant as thick Jersey cream. He reminded me now and then that I really had an easy life.

"Boy, preaching's a snap," he told me one day. "All you need is a Bible and throw together some sermon notes and get up behind the pulpit and shout."

I challenged him then and there to preach in my place the following Sunday. Brashly he accepted, and spent almost every night for a week at our house wading through my library of Bible helps and struggling to put his thoughts down on paper. On Sunday morning he stood in the pulpit and delivered his message. But I detected beads of sweat on the back of his neck as his cockiness wavered and the "cream" grew watery. He never gunned me again about how "preaching is a snap." He did add, however:

"I think every church member ought to preach at least one sermon!"

After moving to Clay Center in 1965 I was elected chairman of the Clay County Ministerial Association, a fellowship of county clergy which I really enjoyed.

This city of some five thousand people wrestled with the problem of its local youth. No longer were our own Methodist young folks content with high school and MYF functions, although they continued in this faithfully. They, together with teenagers of all denominations, congregated wherever they could and lately some of their parties had become quite wild, so we were told.

Late one evening a mother came to the parsonage and told me tearfully that her son was among other teenagers who met in the dingy old Legion Building. She said they were unchaperoned, and sometimes the kids drank something stronger than Cokes.

"Can't you county preachers do something to provide a decent place for the kids of the community to gather?" she asked anxiously.

At the next meeting of our ministerial group I brought the matter up. We discussed the need for a center where the young folks could gather for clean entertainment and refreshments at designated hours of the week.

Bruce Henderson, associate pastor of the First Presbyterian Church, and I began to work with the idea of the youth center. I contacted high schoolers, visiting every class, and asked how many would be interested. The majority were for it. We called a meeting and appointed committees.

At first we considered the matter of purchasing the old Wesleyan Methodist Church building to convert into a meeting place, but this was deemed financially unfeasible. Out of the 500 high schoolers contacted, 250 bought membership tickets at $1.50 each and we decided we had enough finances to begin.

We finally decided on a temporary place and got permission to use the auditorium of the old city hall for the center's temporary headquarters.

Plans buzzed as committees worked to provide entertainment. Among the features were two Ping-Pong tables, three pinball machines, a pool table, plus various other games, ice-cream and soft-drink machines, and a jukebox. The citizens of Clay Center generously helped out.

The kickoff grand opening party was scheduled for Saturday evening on December 31, 1966. Friday night I had finished my sermon and bulletins for Sunday, and as I laid my prepared sermon notes and Bible on the bedroom dresser on Saturday morning I turned to Marilyn.

"I'm going to run down to the Center and give those kids a hand with getting the last-minute things ready for tonight," I told her.

Picking up my coat, I took Vincie with me and we set out together for the auditorium. When Vincie and I arrived the building swarmed with busy teenagers setting up their games, pictures, and lights, and making room for the tables. I hung my coat on a peg and decided to make myself useful.

The night before, another organization had used the

142

building for a meeting and had left the huge cast-iron spotlight weighing 150 pounds on the overhanging balcony, plugged into an outlet below.

I was carrying several folding chairs across the room, feeling particularly good because the Clay County teenagers would at last have a decent place in which to meet. In my preoccupation I failed to see the wires crisscrossing as they hung from the balcony.

Without warning the legs of the folding chairs I was carrying became tangled in the wires. Too late I saw the top-heavy lamp hurtle from its ledge and sail toward me. I tried unsuccessfully to catch it. Instead it came down horribly on the right side of my head and I was knocked into a crumpled heap. I was unaware that thick, wet blood gushed from the hole in my head and soaked the floor around me.

Nor did I hear the anguished cry that swept across the room:

"Oh, God . . . Reverend Paul — is dead. . . ."

BOOK THREE "Miles"

1

The next several days that followed are completely lost to me. Marilyn tells me that the nightmare which was to explode her life into a million pieces gave her no advance warning.

That morning after Vincie and I had left for the city building, she went about her work of planning a company dinner. Ernie Bauer, one of our favorite young people from the Broughton church, was home from college and we eagerly anticipated a time of fellowship with him and his family around the dinner table.

There was a yeasty aroma of bread rising on the top of the stove and Marilyn hummed under her breath as she went to bathe Krassina.

A bit later a group of excited teenage girls from the Youth Center dropped by for some materials. Sitting around in the living room they chattered and giggled as they waited for the rest of their friends.

The jangle of the telephone rudely interrupted the gay visit and Marilyn arose to answer it.

"I'm calling from the city office," a woman's voice said with painful casualness. "It seems that your husband has had an accident. A light bulb fell on his head and he's been taken to the Clay County Hospital."

Marilyn dismissed the mention of the accident almost lightly, for a 100-watt bulb surely couldn't have caused more than a small cut and would need only a few stitches.

She asked one of the girls for a ride to the hospital because the car was not at home. She decided to drop Krassina off at the Wade Bauers who lived across from the hospital and perhaps they could bring her with them when they came for the dinner later.

Minutes after, Marilyn hurried across from the Bauers to the hospital's emergency entrance.

People stood around, their faces carved in stunned disbelief. As Dr. O'Donnell rushed up to her he placed a gentle hand on her shoulders. She sensed a desperate urgency as he spoke.

"It's serious — very serious, Mrs. Miller."

And for the first time Marilyn grew genuinely alarmed. Behind-the-scenes preparations were being made to rush me to Topeka's Stormont-Vail Hospital where I would be under the special care of Dr. Robert Woods, neurosurgeon from the Menninger Foundation.

While waiting for the large ambulance which was to transport me to Topeka, ninety miles away, Marilyn gratefully accepted Bruce Henderson's generous offer to drive her home where she could throw a few clothes into a suitcase so she could accompany me in the ambulance.

"When Bruce first heard," Marilyn says, "he came to me and I sensed his deep sympathy. His eyes were red and bright with unshed tears. As though he wished he could have been on that stretcher in Paul's place. He said he regretted that he hadn't been there at the Center that morning to help."

Our good friend Erma Spellman, who was also a

146

registered nurse, hovered over me anxiously and remarked that it would be a miracle if I lived. Dr. Kelly had already X-rayed my head and set up the intravenous feedings into my system. (Later he was credited with saving my life by this quick action.) He hopped into the ambulance beside me, his arms loaded with necessary emergency equipment.

Don Purling, another family friend, took the steering wheel of the ambulance. As we tore away from the hospital and raced onto the highway, full sirens screaming, Dr. Kelly moved over me with the oxygen mask ready, and his finger on my wrist to monitor my feeble pulse. There were no towels, no cloths, to soak up the blood that gushed from my head and dripped in sticky wet puddles onto the floor.

Don handed back several sticks of gum. "Here. You people better start chewing. It will help." Don himself was under extreme tension because of his close association with us.

Marilyn's eyes clung to the climbing speedometer. When it hit 120 mph, she wondered why it was going so slow!

Snow had blown like tangled confetti across the highways and fields the day before, settling on houses and sheds, and penciling the bare trees with thin white lines. Wet spots still glazed the roads and the State Highway Patrol piloted us the last frantic miles into the state capital.

The accident had occurred at about ten a.m. and by 12:15 the ambulance screamed to a stop at the Stormont-Vail Hospital's emergency entrance.

Still unconscious, I was hurried through the door

and whisked into Emergency. Dr. Kelly, after conferring with the Topeka doctors, took Marilyn into a waiting room reserved for the police and bought her a cup of coffee.

"Do you have any money, Mrs. Miller?" he asked kindly.

She shook her head, for in her confusion she had forgotten to take her purse when she stopped at home to pack. He took out his billfold and shoved all the bills he had — about twelve dollars — into her shaking hands.

"You'll be needing it," he said quietly.

Dr. Woods stepped out of surgery and asked Marilyn if she knew anyone in Topeka who could come to be with her. Again she shook her head in bewilderment.

He immediately put through a call to a friend, Dr. Ewart Watts, the minister of the First Methodist Church of Topeka, who arrived within minutes.

Marilyn had the presence of mind to phone Rev. Howard VonSchriltz of the Clay Center First Methodist Church and told him what was happening in Topeka. Crying brokenly, she made several other necessary calls, including one to my parents in Ohio and one to hers in Michigan.

A Salvation Army lassie, noticing her upset condition, called Bishop McFerrin Stowe and told him about the accident. When Dr. Watts arrived, he proved to be a real boon to Marilyn, and talked to her until time for my surgery which was scheduled at 1:30. During my ordeal in the operating room, others came to be with her, including Mrs. Stowe, Mrs.

Watts, and Rev. Roger Biddle.

Dr. Woods' shoulders sagged with weariness and strain when he came out of surgery two or three hours later.

"About all we've been able to do for your husband, Mrs. Miller, is first aid," he said frankly. "The rest is up to God."

Shortly after, I was wheeled down to the intensive care unit which was on the first floor. By that time our friends had begun to arrive: Rev. Miles Henry of the Marion United Methodist Church; Howard VonSchriltz, the Chris Malls, and Joe and Cathy Haney, all of Clay Center. Prayers, which had begun as trickles, turned to rushing rivers as the group gathered to pray. Mrs. Watts rushed home and came back with soup and sandwiches for Marilyn.

The doctor knew I was critically ill, and the chances for my recovery were remote. Even if I lived, he said, I might never function normally and could become almost a vegetable, probably never to speak or walk again.

No wonder Marilyn was crushed. Our friends' presence buoyed her up immeasurably during that crucial time of waiting. Cathy Haney had thoughtfully picked up some clothes and a purse at the house before coming to Topeka, and Judi Hendersen sent over little things, like perfume, stationery, and Kleenex from time to time.

The group was sitting silent and anxious in the hospital's large lobby when Bishop Stowe arrived. Immediately they sensed a reverent hush as he placed his hand on Marilyn's head and began to pray

— beautifully and compassionately, as he talked with the heavenly Father. Someone remarked that one could *feel* the Power entering the room during this time of prayer. It seemed that everyone present, including Marilyn, was aware of the comforting presence of the Holy Spirit.

"I have never heard a more meaningful, more touching prayer," she recalls.

The group in the waiting room literally bombarded God's merciful throne with petitions to spare my life for His glory and honor. Yet never did anyone pray *only* for my recovery. It was always that I might continue to serve Him.

As the group was praying, Mr. Roberts, the male attendant, came running into the waiting room.

"Mrs. Miller! Mrs. Miller, come quick! Your husband's trying to say something!" he almost shouted. She followed him hastily into the intensive care ward.

I'd been wrapped in blackness, velvety and obscure. Now something twisted and tortured and bewildered me — something struggling to exist, to emerge. Something writhing and nauseated and moaning, shot with a shower of hot sparks. I groped, wheeling over the pit of the dark, for it was agony to be only a speck. . . . Then in a blur I saw Marilyn's face, tears cutting shiny paths across it, and I said it again — faintly:

"Dit-to. . . ."

"Ditto!" Marilyn was sobbing out loud now. "Oh — Paul. . . ." She recognized our code for "I love you" even in the thickness of my garbled, labored speech.

Tears streaming down her cheeks, she ran from the room and flew excitedly to our friends in the waiting room.

"Paul. . . ," she choked on her tears. "Paul —
talked. He — remembered our secret code for 'I love
you.' It means — " she paused to swallow her sobs
— "his memory is all right. . . ."

However, my groping out of the darkness was
brief, and minutes later I lapsed back into unconsciousness.

2

Marilyn sat through the long, endless hours in the waiting room. Miles Henry and Howard VonSchriltz remained with her, reading Scripture after Scripture and praying long and earnestly for me.

The hours following New Year's Eve with its wild revelry, its dull clangor of midnight bells, and honking horns became a nightmare. Ambulances streamed in and out constantly all night with sirens blowing, bringing in the victims of accidents which were caused by drunken driving.

"I thought I couldn't stand it," Marilyn said, "seeing the harrowing fear in the eyes of the people who waited for their loved ones to come out of emergency."

One young man was brought into the intensive care ward after having run off the road and being pinned beneath his car. His agonizing screams pierced the halls as he cried out in his delirium:

"Help! Help me out of the ditch. . . ."

Marilyn was permitted to catch only brief glimpses of me through the small glass pane in the intensive care room door, for the doctor had told her it would be at least twenty-four to forty-eight hours before they would know if I would live.

Dr. and Mrs. Watts came by after their watch-night service in church and asked Marilyn to go home with them, but she felt she couldn't leave the hospital.

152

The long, grueling hours of waiting and the drama of horror that continued through the endless night had exhausted her. In the morning she gave in. She and the two preacher-friends went to the Watts' for breakfast.

Since there was little change in my condition in the morning, Howard decided to drive back to Clay Center, but Miles stayed.

On Sunday afternoon my parents arrived, along with my brother Fred and sister Evalee, having driven straight through from Ohio since New Year's Eve. They were shocked at my condition. My head was swollen almost twice its normal size and was heavily bandaged; my left eye, which had bulged out from the accident now bore ugly blue-black marks. My mouth was drawn upward in a horrible grimace.

Marilyn, Mom, and Dad took turns in seeing me very briefly from time to time, but Mom took it exceptionally hard. They were forced to drive back to Ohio on Monday afternoon, for Dad and my brother, who had brought them, had to be back at work. They wondered if they would ever see me again.

Marilyn's parents and her sister Marge came on Monday. After seeing me, they drove to Clay Center to our house and stayed with the children. Marge came back with Howard VonSchriltz to be with Marilyn for a week.

Howard brought most unusual news, "Marilyn, those kids canceled their grand opening. When they learned about the seriousness of Paul's injuries they all spent New Year's Eve in their churches on their knees, praying for his recovery." It touched her deeply.

Bruce had posted the following notice on the chapel door of his church:

INFORMATION CONCERNING PAUL MILLER:

From a telephone conversation with Mrs. Miller late this afternoon, the report concerning Paul Miller is that his condition is very serious. Following an operation, he was taken to the intensive care unit of the hospital in Topeka where he remains unconscious.

The doctor predicts that he may not regain consciousness for over 48 hours. It will be some time after that before they will be able to determine the extent of his injury. There is the possibility of brain damage. How serious the damage may be is not known.

Please use the Junior Chapel for a time of prayer on behalf of Reverend Miller and his family. The Christian faith goes beyond our understanding and our ability to reason. Therefore, pray.

For two nights Marilyn slept at the Watts' in the parsonage. Then the administrator for the Methodist Home for the Aged came and offered her a room there, which was a scant four blocks from the hospital.

During her stay in the waiting room with Marge beside her, and our minister-friends dropping by constantly to pray, she became acquainted with many people who also had loved ones in the intensive care unit with me. A strong bond of fellowship developed.

"In the bed next to Paul lay a man," Marilyn recalls, "who had fallen down the basement steps, and became unconscious from a concussion and was near death. His family was with him constantly, and one time when I was with Paul, this man's aunt was in the room too.

154

"By this time Paul had come to a little. We had no idea what their religious background was, but Paul said just before she left the room: 'Will you join my wife in the chapel and pray for me and light a candle?' Now, how could Paul have known she was a Catholic?"

Marilyn and this woman went to pray — each in her own way — a Protestant and a Catholic, reaching out to God together!

For me, dreams and unconsciousness came and went like lazy waves rolling upon the sands.

One day during one of my delirious moments, I was sure I'd seen an unorthodox situation.

"Get that big German police dog out of here!" I yelled. "He's lapping up the intraveneous fluid that's spilling from my bottle!"

The poor bewildered nurse tried her best to convince me that there was no dog in the ward.

When the person next to me lay dying, I overheard the doctors and nurses speaking in hushed tones about death. So convinced was I that they were talking about me that I stopped breathing. They had to administer oxygen to revive me.

They tell me I was constantly praying for the other patients in the intensive care ward when it wasn't even certain that I myself would live. Marilyn says that with my preacher-friends coming in to pray, it seemed as though Jesus Himself walked along the corridors of the unit.

One day Dr. Woods said to me, "Frankly, I was curious as to what a preacher would say under the anesthetic. I've heard some pretty blistering language from some young patients on the operating table."

155

Although I was unable to speak during the operation, I now quoted parts of Psalm 27: "The Lord is my light and my salvation; whom shall I fear? the Lord is the strength of my life; of whom shall I be afraid?"

Miles Henry came as often as he could, and was a real inspiration to us. I was conscious most of the time now, and he spent as much time as he was able, praying and reading the Bible to me.

At one time one of the nurses almost threw Miles out because he and I would get so carried away that we'd break into a song or psalm, not cognizant of the fact that there were others in the ward. I quoted psalms verbatim, which I didn't realize I knew from memory.

Miles recalls: "One day, right there in intensive care, Paul asked me to sing *The Lord Is My Light*. I thought we surely couldn't get by with that. I hesitated. He said, 'Come on; I'll sing it with you.' Paul never bragged about his singing. In fact, he threatens people with it! It was beautiful!"

During those first days after my surgery I had an unforgettable vision. It seemed I was about to enter heaven. The light from that temple-domed, steeple-studded city was so bright that it was as if all the lights of the earth were turned on at once! As I stood transfixed by this awesome sight, the word LIFE in gigantic letters floated toward me, and I wanted desperately to throw off the confining fetters of my feeble body and run into its light-saturated streets! But before I could break away it faded from sight. God gave me a glimpse of the glory which is to come. For some reason I wasn't yet permitted to enter in. But it was worth going through all the suffering just to see that vision.

In another vision I was lying in a casket at the Ebenezer church. As I heard the congregation singing joyful songs I grew thirsty. Mert Schwenson, the funeral director from Clay Center, stooped over to offer me a drink.

When the scene vanished I became obsessed with the thought of death. I turned to Howard Von-Schriltz:

"I don't think I'll make it, Howard," I said in a melancholy voice. "Please take care of Marilyn and the children — after I'm gone. And you will preach at my funeral, won't you?"

"I will not," Howard replied positively, "because you're not going to die!"

But they tell me I talked continually of my own funeral after that, and by Tuesday night following the accident I had everyone worried. I even asked Marilyn to get young Johnny Starkweather to play his drums at my funeral. Maybe he could pound out something religious, I said.

Marilyn sat at my bedside and whispered through her tears. "Paul . . . Paul, I need you — the children need you — God's people need you — you can't leave us now!"

Because of the precariousness of my condition, my legs and my right hand had to be tied to the bed. I was fully convinced that the nurses were abusing me and I begged Marilyn to have me transferred to the Clay County Hospital. She was willing to do anything

157

for my peace of mind, and in her desperation she buttonholed Dr. Woods and begged him almost hysterically to release me.

Dr. Woods tried to tell her that I was receiving excellent care and that the nurses were doing only what was best for me. When she realized that he was right, she was embarrassed at her outburst.

Marilyn tells how she spent many hours in the chapel, crying and praying. She had been under such tension and was so overwhelmingly shaken up by this whole nightmarish ordeal that she pleaded with God to spare my life.

"But when I finally began to pray that God's will be done, and relinquished my hold on Paul's life and turned everything completely over to Him, Paul began to improve slowly," she recalls with an odd catch in her voice. "Suddenly a feeling of peace fell over me — a 'peace . . . which passeth all understanding' — and I knew I could take whatever He would send."

One day the doctor took her aside and gave her news that would have shattered the average person.

"Your husband, Mrs. Miller, will never preach again, I'm afraid. What provisions do you have by the way of insurance to care for yourself and your children?"

She had gradually come to realize the seriousness of my condition, but to hear it from the doctor's own lips made it horribly real. Realizing that I might never function normally again, she felt crushed at first. But God became so very precious to her at that time that she was able to bear up under the strain in a remarkable way.

She mentioned it to Howard one day, who grabbed Dr. Woods' coat lapels and asked him point-blank:

"What are Paul Miller's chances? We've got to know!"

The doctor hesitated only a moment. "He will never walk behind his pulpit again. There's far too much brain damage for that. In other words, his ministry is over."

But God had other plans.

Lying gravely ill next to me, a man was about to stop breathing. I don't remember it, but they tell me I reached out my hand toward him. As I moved my hand up and down, and while I prayed and praised, the man's chest began to rise and fall in rhythm. Soon he was breathing again.

During my nineteen-day stay in the intensive care ward I talked to many people. In a letter sent by a woman whose father lay beside me in the unit, she wrote to her cousin in Beloit:

> At the time Pop was in intensive care a Methodist minister from Clay Center was there too. His case is truly a miracle. By the time he was taken to another floor he and his wife had become a great blessing to many people.
>
> Mrs. Miller told us one day he asked the doctor how a man next to him was doing and when the doctor told him the man was better, he said, 'Good. I have been praying for him,' and with that he started singing, 'Praise God from whom all blessings flow. . . .''
>
> As relatives (of those who were brought into the intensive care ward) gathered in the waiting room, Mrs. Miller would talk to those who were crying and tell

them what God had done for her husband and ask if she might pray for their loved ones. She gave several faith to hold on and put smiles on their faces. Rev. Miller was so sick himself but it was heartwarming to hear he was praying for the others beside him. Yesterday she told us he is getting better each day. That is truly an answer to prayer.

The next notice on Bruce Henderson's chapel door went like this:

A 7:30 p.m. phone call from Topeka has brought encouraging news. Unexpectedly Paul became conscious enough to say a few words!! This was more than anyone had thought possible tonight. Keep praying. With God nothing is impossible!

I had announced to everyone that I was going to get up and preach in my churches on Easter Sunday. Some of the hospital staff tried to humor me. They'd smile knowingly and say,

"Maybe some Easter."

But I never lost faith in the goal I'd set for myself, for I meant March 26, 1967.

Marilyn was a blessing wherever she went, as she talked to people. God led her and the ministers who came to visit me to speak to those in the waiting room and comfort them. There were some definite answers to prayer as a result.

Because I had no feeling on the left side of my body, it was feared I would be paralyzed for life. The doctors carried pins with them and pricked me every chance they got. Dr. Tozier, who was Dr. Woods' associate, peppered his conversation with a great deal of profanity. He'd take his pin and prick me and then he would say:

"Do you feel that d— —n pin?"

I had heard his pet word so much that subconsciously I absorbed it. Once while I lapsed into one of my earlier delirious spells I yelled after one of his pin-pricks:

"Yes, and if you don't stop sticking those d— —n pins into me I'll kick you in the face!"

I had always been known for my hearty laughter and ready wit, and now my face was drawn into Gargantuan features. I remember catching a glimpse of myself in a mirror during therapy one day. When I realized that I was the creature looking like a frightened baboon, I broke down and cried. It was to take months before I could laugh normally again. Gradually my sense of humor returned too.

At first my visitors were limited to the members of the family. When I saw my good friend Leo Chapman's face in the small glass pane of the door I knew they wouldn't let him in. But Leo was good for me, so I called out:

"Hi, *Uncle Leo!*" They let him in to see me.

When Leo came through the door he rubbed the back of his hand across his nose and in his droll way, he muttered,

"Sorry to hear you were injured, Reverend Paul. When I heard you were hit on the head I quit worrying." Which sounded exactly like Leo!

Bud Neill and Mert Schwenson, our Clay Center morticians, came in for a short visit. I grinned at them lopsidedly and cracked,

"Well, I cheated the two of you out of a funeral,

didn't I?"

They roared with laughter. But not everything was funny.

One day Marilyn brought the children to Topeka to see me. They had looked forward eagerly to the visit, for they hadn't seen me for about three weeks. When I was wheeled into the intensive care waiting room I saw their happy faces turn to horror. Kassie turned and ran sobbing from the room.

Small wonder. My head was still bandaged, with my ears popping out like opened car doors; and the left side of my mouth was tightly drawn up in an inhuman grimace. It was a traumatic experience for the children, and one they didn't soon forget.

3

Marilyn and I debated what to do about my hospitalization expenses. This matter became extremely urgent after we learned that our insurance company had canceled our coverage. While this subject was still fresh in our minds, Representative Fred Meek from Clay County dropped in for a visit. Since I was a Navy veteran, we broached the idea which we had considered about my going to the Veteran's Hospital in Topeka. He was sympathetic and eager to see what he could do to help. He even took Marilyn along to the VA hospital while making inquiries.

"It could take months before all the red tape is unsnarled," we were told.

Months! The time might as well have been years, for we could scarcely afford hospital care for another day, much less longer than that.

But the Austrian hymn says: "[God] never cometh late," and in a few days the wheels were set in motion, and to our surprise I was loaded into an ambulance and transferred across town to the massive, staid government hospital.

Arriving there, I was taken down one long corridor after another, past the nurses' station, and then down a hall which opened off into a number of private rooms. Finally we reached Ward I-5A.

"This is where you'll be staying, Mr. Miller," one

163

of the friendly nurses told me.

As they lifted me into my bed near the door, I threw a quick look around the ward. The horrible stench of uncontrolled bladders and bowels rushed to my nostrils and I almost gagged. Then I noticed the six men around me. Drawn, haggard faces, hopeless to the point of nausea, they stared with eyes that looked like holes burnt in parchment. As vegetables, they lay in various degrees of being alive, waiting for the clammy hand of death. I cringed at the sight.

There was the man next to my bed with the severed spine. The alcoholic whose excessive imbibing had destroyed his brain. The young man whose skull was crushed when a car fell on his head and who did nothing all day but hold his family's picture before his eyes and mumble. The man with an incurable disease.

And the rest. They looked so hopeless, so forlorn. Heartsick, I shook my head at the nurse.

"Ma'am, I don't like the looks of this," I said jadedly. "These fellas are all candidates for an appointment with the undertaker!"

She turned to me and said frankly, "Mr. Miller, you might as well get used to all this, because you'll have to be here at least three years."

Three years! Why, this was a fate worse than death! As righteous anger overwhelmed me I whirled on her.

"No, Ma'am! I don't care what you say. I'm going to preach in my two churches on Easter Sunday. And that's just a few months away!"

She gave me a benevolent smile and walked away. I began to jot down notes for my Easter sermon.

Marilyn saw the frustration, the hurt, and the fear mirrored in my eyes and she left the room and cried for me. Tearfully she called Mrs. Stowe. In her compassionate manner the bishop's wife listened as Marilyn shared her heartbreaking story, then drove her back to the Methodist Home. Marilyn had wondered if perhaps I wasn't doing as well as we'd thought I was. Yet this experience was psychologically good for me, for it provided me with the incentive to get out of the place as soon as possible.

Presently the doctors came and introduced themselves: Dr. Beard, a big, warmhearted bear of a man came first; and then there was Dr. Rout, a handsome, promising young physician. My first day at the hospital was frankly discouraging.

When Marilyn came back that evening to visit me I was quite upset. If it weren't for her love, and the love of my children and the concern and prayers of hundreds of friends, I think I would have given up. It seemed so futile.

For about three weeks I was confined to my bed. Because of catheters and bedpans, the stench in the ward became overbearing. I'd smother my body with shaving lotion and talcum powder to make it more tolerable. Finally someone put a fan in my corner to blow away some of the foul odor.

Two of the attendants, Bob Taylor and "Brother" Atkinson, became my closest friends. Faces black as ebony, they brightened the gloomy days ahead for me. The candy stripers, Red Cross volunteers, and the "gray ladies" boosted my morale with their helping-hand visits. Mrs. Lindley was my favorite.

165

As I saw some of the patients lifted into wheel-chairs or taking a first walk with a cane or walker, I became impatient and almost envious. When would my turn come? When would I learn to walk so that I could go home?

My all-consuming desire to walk again became almost an obsession with me, and I brooded during the long, wakeful nights. One night I fell asleep and in a dream I was going home. So real was it that I stumbled out of bed and sat down to put on my shoes. As I tried to walk, I fell to the cold, gray-tiled floor and awoke with a start.

"Help!" I yelled, fear washing over me in great waves.

Brother Atkinson was at my side in a moment. "Brother Miller, what do you think you're doing out of bed anyhow?" he demanded. (We had become good friends and since he was a fellow-believer, we called each other "brother.")

I told him of my vivid dream about going home. Of course, he was forced to report the incident and from then on the doctors ordered a restraining belt around my arms to keep me in bed. They realized that another fall like this could be deadly injurious to my head wound, and they were forced to take extra precautions so it wouldn't happen again.

But in my frustration I couldn't understand it and I detested that belt. I was afraid of it because it imprisoned and suffocated me, and I became almost hysterical under its confinement. I yanked and pulled until finally I broke it. I flung it as far out as I could throw it.

Brother Atkinson came and put it back on. During the sleepless night I ripped it off again. This battle went on until Brother Atkinson faced me sternly.

"Brother Miller, you're going to get me into trouble! Know what my wife does when she's afraid? She prays."

Suddenly I could relax and grin. "Hey, that's good advice for a preacher," I cracked.

The next day I made a bargain with the doctors. I wouldn't get out of bed again if they'd remove the belt, and they agreed.

The doctors at the Menninger Foundation were available for consultation, and after I had been at the VA hospital for several days, Dr. Segerson came to see me.

After they had wheeled me into the consultation room, the doctor asked me to draw a picture of a man on the blackboard.

Laboriously I sketched the head of what looked like an African native, and I laid down the chalk.

He looked at it and said, "Is this all there is to a man?"

I looked at my artwork again and realized what I'd done. Now, why had I omitted the man's body? *Is this all there's going to be of me — just a bloody head, an injured brain that can't even function completely?*

Dumbly I heard the doctors reaffirm the fact that I was completely paralyzed on the left side.

I took the chalk and drew a body for the head.

My impatience at the inaction mounted, and I couldn't wait to begin therapy. I wanted to walk so desperately.

167

My first trip to the therapy room was an experience in itself. Pete, Miss Rausch, Johnny, and Marge emanated warmth and cheerfulness. My eyes caught the figure of an elderly man strapped to an electric bicycle which was really making his legs work. This is what I wanted — what I needed.

"Wish I could do that," I thought. I strained and pricked with excitement. But it was to take days before I was ready for that.

I was happy when I graduated into a wheelchair and could struggle along the corridors by myself. It squeaked and clanked in protest — until one day I doused it generously with hair oil which I found in the washroom.

The day I set my feet between the parallel bars and inched my way down its length was a gold-letter day to me. I was walking again! Then I caught sight of myself in the mirror positioned at the other end. Seeing my bandaged head, my face muscles drawn to one side, and my lifeless limbs, I felt like crawling into a crack in the floor and never showing myself again. But my dismay lasted only briefly, for I discovered that as I thanked God for each feeble step instead of feeling sorry for myself, I began to walk better.

I chafed at my impatience to spend more time in the therapy room because it seemed so short. At this rate it would take far too long to walk again. So I devised a clever scheme whereby I could lengthen my walking time. At night I slipped into my wheelchair (it wasn't squeaking now, fortunately!), wheeled myself into the elevator, and went to the hospital chapel on the third floor. Then I locked the wheels on the chair, worked my way out of it, and practiced walking along the pews! I tried several times to kneel at the altar but it was too hard to lower myself to my knees. God was with me in my chair just the same.

One day a man from the Social Security office visited me. He handed me a scrap of paper.

"Here. Sign this," he said.

"What for?" I demanded suspiciously.

"After you've been here for six months," he explained carefully, "you can draw disability insurance. The time to work with that is now."

I refused steadfastly. "I'll be out of here long before the six months are over," I predicted. He eyed me curiously and left.

After the results of a brain wave test had been read, Dr. Rout came to talk to me.

"There are indications that you may be susceptible to seizures and convulsions, and as a precaution we're going to prescribe an anticonvulsant drug for you."

The words stunned me. Now I had visions of standing in my pulpit one minute, and lying prone on the floor the next, frothing at the mouth.

It wasn't right, I screamed inwardly. Here I was progressing reasonably well, and then to have the ministry snatched away from me after all.

"It just isn't fair!" I shouted. "How can I ever preach again?"

That night this fear haunted me and I tossed restlessly. The nurse on duty noticed my turbulent mood and asked what was bothering me. When I told her, she seated herself at my bedside and for a long time

169

she tried to console me.

"A convulsion or a seizure may be only a twitch of the eye or a jerk of the finger, you know," she said.

Relieved, I finally dropped off to sleep.

The new drug made me feel doped and half-asleep all the time. When I complained about this, the doctor cut the dosage from three tablets to one. Even then I felt listless, and decided I could do without it. I had been eating in the dining hall for some time and managed to drop my pill into the empty milk carton from which I drank. I felt much better after that.

Inwardly I was learning to laugh again. My facial muscles were still frozen into an inhuman mispropor-tion. Even though I began to joke and chuckle, I could *say* the ha-ha-ha, but I couldn't smile! Can you imagine laughing with a cold sober look on your face?

Marilyn had brought pictures of each of the children to the hospital and placed them on my bedside table. I often looked at their faces and tried to copy their happy smiles. It was agony not to be home with them.

Yet so determined was I to recover that when staff members would tell me what I might be able to do in two months, I generally had accomplished in two weeks!

Three weeks had gone by since Dr. Segerson's initial examination. When he came back to the VA hospital for another consultation, I was already walking some with only the aid of a cane. My doctors and the attendants decided to surprise him. I was wheeled to the door of the consultation room, and as Brother Atkinson opened the door, I took my cane and walked slowly into the room.

The good doctor's mouth dropped open in surprise

and I was afraid his teeth would fall out. As I reached the middle of the room, I looked for a chair and sat down.

Quickly he retained his composure and asked me what I had planned for myself.

"Throw away this cane," I said confidently, "and walk into my pulpit and preach."

"Keep up the good work," he said nonchalantly, but I caught the twinkle of his eyes.

4

The stream of visitors to Ward I-5A for me seemed constant. When the number exceeded forty in one given day, the nurse put her foot down.

"This isn't a social club, Mr. Miller," she said flatly.

For a week I wasn't permitted to see anyone but Marilyn. Whenever I saw her coming down the long hall, I'd race past the private rooms in my wheelchair to meet her. She was like a drink of fresh water to my dreary desert existence.

My mail reached staggering proportions, for in all my weeks' stay in the hospital I received over six hundred cards and letters from friends and relatives, and even from strangers. I felt sorry for the forgotten fellows in my ward whenever the mailman came, for it seemed he literally dumped out his sack with mail for me. The staff used to josh me by saying they had to hire a special carrier just for me!

After I was permitted to have visitors again, several of my young church people came in, including Ernie Bauer.

Sitting in my wheelchair, I was disturbed to see Ernie take out his lighter and light a cigarette. He knew I disapproved of smoking but it had become an unshakable habit with him.

I pointed to a fellow-patient who gasped and racked with emphysema.

"Look, Ernie. That's what might happen to you, if you don't kick the habit," I told him gravely.

He nodded. "Yeah. I know."

"Tell you what," he went on after a thoughtful silence. "I'll quit smoking the day you start walking."

"OK, Ernie. It's a deal," I said, and shook his hand on it.

Some weeks later I was walking with only the help of a cane.

When I had been in the hospital for three or four weeks I buttonholed Dr. Beard in the hall and asked him if he'd do me a favor.

"Sure. I will if I can," he said pleasantly.

"I'd like to go home next weekend," I said boldly.

"What! Go home? Just who do you think," he said tartly, "would turn you over every hour on the hour?"

My dander was up. "Listen, Doc. I've been turning myself ever since I got here!"

He seemed almost more surprised than the time when he walked up to my bed one morning. This was after Miles Henry had been over and we had prayed about the inability to move my left leg. Two days later I was able to swing it freely. That day when I met him with, "Look, Doc," and kicked my leg into the air, he was almost knocked speechless.

After verifying that I didn't have to be turned he gave me permission to go home for Friday night only. I tried to talk him into letting me stay for two nights, but he was adamant.

"One night only. Unless the weather turns bad," he added.

"I'm going to pray for a blizzard," I told one of the therapists later. For, of course, the doctor didn't want me to risk my life if it snowed.

I was as excited at the prospect of going home as a kid with a circus, and could hardly wait until Miles and Paula came to pick me up. This was going to be the first time in 2 1/2 months that I was to be back at the parsonage. Far ahead of time I sat dressed and waiting, and it seemed like hours before I saw my friends coming down the corridor for me.

Clay County never looked better than that raw March afternoon as the car purred down the highway and finally into the county seat where we lived. At long last it pulled up before the parsonage. The children had fashioned a heartwarming, though a bit lopsided sign which read: WELCOME HOME, DAD, and taped it across the front door.

As I hobbled up the porch my eyes blurred, for it was something akin to heaven when I stepped inside the door. Wearing my antiseptic green skullcap to protect my head wound, I must have looked strange to the children, for my mouth still pulled up to one side. But they didn't let on. They hugged me tight in their happiness to see me.

With the family showering me with all their love and attention and the favorite foods Marilyn had prepared, I tried to relax. But all the excitement and the long, tiring ride grated on my nerves and they grew raw. Without being able to control myself I screamed at the kids when they dropped silverware or became too boisterous.

Being home was harder on Marilyn than she liked

to admit. Every time I dropped my cane her heart flew to her throat, for she was afraid I had fallen. All my painful progress could be wiped out in one misstep if my head wound reopened.

In spite of all the tensions, I dreaded for morning to come and I would have to return to the hospital. But when Saturday dawned, a light thin snow had fallen. Howard VonSchriltz called the hospital and reported that Clay Center was having snow, and that I wouldn't be back until Sunday afternoon.

When I got back, I cornered Dr. Rout. "About that snowstorm," I said dryly. "We had about twelve flakes!"

He eyed me suspiciously. "That was a h— — — of a snowstorn, wasn't it?"

The therapists wouldn't let me hear the end of it, and one of them said that if he ever wanted anything from God he knew whom to see.

"You've got the right connections!" he added.

My next trip home was over the weekend. This time I wore a white crash protection helmet. When Howard and I decided to stop downtown for a cup of coffee, I created quite a stir as I stepped from the car at the cafe, wearing the helmet and carrying my cane. A car screeched to a stop as the driver sat and stared at me fully two minutes before driving on!

When we stopped at Marshall's Chrysler-Plymouth Motors, my friends jotted on my helmet: "The good guy in the white hat."

That Sunday I went to the Ebenezer church. I wore my sterilized skullcap and slipped into a pew near the back. I guess I looked worse than I figured, for a man fainted after he saw me and had to be helped out.

Glenn Claycamp, a lay speaker, preached the sermon that morning. As I sat in that pew and listened I wondered what it would be like to stand behind my pulpit once more. Would God see fit to use me again?

After church there was much backslapping and hand-pumping and well-wishing. I don't think anyone passed me by!

On one of my weekends home I was asked to visit the Youth Center which had opened in late January. With help, I had staggered up two flights of stairs, and when I was ushered through the swinging doors, the band struck up the music and the kids burst into "For He's a Jolly Good Fellow." Across the stage a huge, neatly lettered banner read: WE'RE GLAD YOU'RE BACK, REVEREND PAUL. When the music stopped I was asked to say a word to them.

Blinking back the tears, I moved a few steps forward to the microphone and said huskily:

"You've heard recently that 'God is dead,' or that He doesn't exist. But I stand before you tonight as a living witness that God is not dead; that He does exist. And He has heard and answered your prayers. Thank you."

There was hardly a dry eye in the room. The moment touched me deeply.

One raw March weekend I decided to attend the regional basketball tournament. Wearing my helmet and big black high shoes (to protect my left ankle) I thumped into the gym. The Clay Center *Dispatch* had this to say about my presence:

> "Some may have thought the special feature of the regional tournament last Saturday was the appearance of

Clay Center's team but so far as we were concerned, it was the fact that the Rev. Paul Miller came walking in. That was the big feature of the tournament. We sort of had the feeling all along that the Clay Center boys were going to be there Saturday night but we surely had not thought the Reverend Miller would be."

One weekend I was all set to go home and dressed and waiting in the hall. Marilyn and our friends, Wallace and Leota Fowles, had arrived to take me. I needed only to pick up my pass at the desk.

After thumbing through a sheaf of papers the nurse on duty shook her smartly coiffed head.

"I'm sorry, Mr. Miller, but I can't seem to find your pass."

I distinctly remembered having asked the doctor in charge to sign the pass, but in his absorption he must have forgotten. Since this was after hours, all the doctors had left the hospital. When I realized that I couldn't go home unless I had the pass, I became panic-stricken.

Tears streamed down my face — for I hadn't yet learned to control my emotions — and I yelled:

"I'm going home and if I have to crawl all the way to Clay Center!"

"I'm sorry. . . ," she said again, "but rules are rules."

Her words seemed so cold, so heartless, but they could make no exceptions for me, she said. Finally she did round up the doctor and I didn't need to crawl home after all. I went happily by car.

During those weekends when I was unable to go home, I grew bored and impatient.

One day a new friend promised to teach me how to sculpt. If I would come to his ward he'd show me how, he said. Anything to pass the long, lonely hours, I thought, and so we made our plans.

The strict, redheaded nurse, however, had other ideas. She refused to let me go. I said I'd go anyhow, but she was firm.

Frustrated and angry, I was ready to burst into tears.

"I want out of here," I stormed, "and you can't keep me!"

She had her hands full trying to persuade me to calm down but I stubbornly resisted.

Just then the door opened and the Morris Toopers from Kankakee walked in. It had been some time since I had seen these old friends and their visit was exactly what I needed to restore my equilibrium.

Miles Henry always came at the right time, too. He brought me a large-print New Testament and I spent a great deal of time reading and meditating upon God's Word. One earlier time before I was permitted to go home I attended services in the hospital chapel. I saw the other communicants go forward and kneel at the altar and partake of the bread and the cup. I was unable to go to the altar, but was served the elements while in my wheelchair. Remembering the Christ who died for me enriched me spiritually that week.

Because I often wheeled myself around the wards and talked to the other patients of Jesus Christ, the nurses said my being there was a real ministry to the men. Brother Atkinson began to call me "Sunshine." Sometimes my laughter nearly wore the others out, for when I started to laugh I could hardly stop.

Yet often when I went to pray for the patients I would feel frustrated. Here they were, hopeless and in despair, and I was getting well. Why couldn't God give them the same surging health and strength He was giving to me?

In spite of my own pain I laughed my way around the hospital. With my skullcap on my head and my elastic bandage on my left leg, I was making tremendous headways.

A melancholy veteran who had come in for treatment gave me a morose scowl one morning.

"You look like terrible, man. What do you have to be happy about?" he muttered.

"Look," I told him, "if you'd have seen me two months ago you'd know why!"

I wanted desperately to be released from the hospital and grew more impatient than ever to walk again. Somehow the pitifully handicapped Jane Merchant's poem became very real to me then, for it expressed my feelings so well. I had used it often in my sermons. It follows:

"Full half-a-hundred timed I've sobbed,
'I can't go on, I can't go on.'
And yet full half-a-hundred times
I've hushed my sobs, and gone.
My answer, if you ask me how,
May seem presumptuously odd,
But I think that what kept me keeping on
When I could not, was God."°

° From *Halfway Up the Sky* by Jane Merchant. Copyright 1956 Southern Publishing Association. Used by permission of Abingdon Press.

5

It was God! In everything we saw His guiding hand, and we had to admit over and over that we dared do "all things" through Him. So many things had proved this.

It was God, when people rushed in and stood by and encouraged us through the following, long weary months after the accident with their prayers, their help, and their gifts.

Dr. O. Ray Cook, superintendent of the Concordia district of the Methodist Church, took over my ministerial duties at both of my churches. He wrote to us after the first Sunday:

> Everything went well at the churches yesterday in spite of the preacher and the zero weather which seemed to wreak its vengeance on the Hayes church. You see, the line evidently froze to the furnace so that when we arrived the temperature in the sanctuary was 50 degrees. . . . The Pastoral Relations Committee met at Ebenezer and it was decided to ask Glenn Claycamp to fill in for you until you come back. This fitted the wishes of the Hayes people too. They will work out a remuneration for Glenn. So there is nothing for you to worry about. . . . Wherever we go, Paul, people are inquiring of your condition. You are a well-publicized individual. Maybe you will get to be bishop! Ha.

When we were informed that our hospital insurance had been canceled due to a technicality, and our bank balance — which never seemed to swell more than knee-high to a hoptoad — was nearly depleted, Marilyn's thoughts must have raced in circles, trying to decide how to manage. Dr. Cook helped her with the financial arrangements of the hospital and lifted a heavy weight from her sturdy shoulders.

From the very first hour in the hospital when Dr. Kelly pressed his twelve dollars into Marilyn's hand, until April 13, nearly $6,000 later, "it was God" who saw that our needs were met.

But more than that, we received hundreds of letters of encouragement from people all over who told us they were remembering us. In nearly every instance there was a check enclosed, or a handful of bills, to "give feet to their faith."

Their love and devotion to us and our Lord simply staggered our comprehension, and the very spontaneity of it overwhelmed us.

For the first several days while I lay in the intensive care unit, Marilyn received many phone calls from concerned relatives and friends. In fact, the receptionist became rather irked because she seemed to get little else done besides "paging Mrs. Miller — telephone!"

We can't begin to share all the words of compassion and cheer which we received during that trying ordeal — they would have filled volumes — but a sampling follows:

Our friends, the Chris Malls, who had come right to Topeka with the Haneys the night of the accident, wrote later:

Everyone who prays remembers Paul and you in their prayers. Many churches besides ours have held prayer services for the Millers. It makes us all feel nice that other folks appreciate you two as we do. . . .

I'd counseled with Larry and Tana some time back and they had become very dear to us. In fact, we weren't quite sure where they stood spiritually until they wrote to us. In her letter to us, Tana said:

There aren't words enough to express how we feel, and of course, we wonder why of all people this had to happen to Paul. Larry said it must be a part of God's plan as there is no other explanation. . . . We want to do something. If there is anything — if you need us, just ask us. We'll drop everything to come to Clay or Topeka. . . . We haven't told either of you this, but Paul saved our life. That's the only way to put it . . . he really straightened out our way of thinking. . . . Our thoughts and our prayers will be constantly with you. . . .

In a letter from a woman whom we had never met (and there were many others), we were heartened when she told us:

I read of your misfortune in the paper and now of your wonderful recovery. During my life I have experienced many things and I sincerely believe 'Faith is the substance of all things possible.' I feel especially blessed to be up and going and in that spirit I want to contribute a little gift. . . .

A hundred dollar check was enclosed.

Judi Henderson often sent notes to Marilyn, written in her fine script, and her words throbbed with "loving empathy," as she worded it.

182

We're so grateful for any encouraging news and we pray it will continue that way with hope and strength. Paul will be helping God help him recover.

We heard from Ada too.

I don't think Paul realized how much he did for me when Les passed away. Les loved him too, and we felt he was almost like one of our own kids. . . . I am praying for Paul and you. . . . Don't hesitate to call on the kids (in Topeka) if you need anything.

The following letter written to Howard VonSchriltz by an anonymous layman was shared with the readers of the Clay County Co-Op Newsletter, in the issue of January 1967:

It seems to me there are too few men patting their earth with the bottoms of their feet, who impress me with their sincerity and genuine love for their fellowmen. I've recognized it in your friend Paul Miller. Combined with his quick response to humorous and friendly overtures, I consider him endowed with a warmth that should prove him very valuable to his calling, his church, and to mankind in general.

For the sake of his family and friends as well as the community at large, I hope he makes a complete and speedy recovery; for I'm wishing for an early excuse to offer my prayers of gratitude for the fulfillment of that hope. . . .

Another letter, written on January 9, came to me from our friend Sister Ann-Loretta, of Manhattan:

I was shocked and sorry to hear of your accident. You may rest assured that I will storm heaven with my prayers for your complete recovery. The Sisters are all praying for you also.

183

Truly, love and concern knows no religious barriers! Leota Fowles wrote:

> We are thinking of you constantly and waiting for the telephone to ring, telling us of good news about Paul. If you think of anything you want us to do, don't be afraid to ask. Call us collect as all are anxious to hear.

Our friends, Herb and L'Jeane wrote:

> Words seem so inadequate at times like these, but we both want both of you to know that you and your children are in our constant thoughts and prayers at this trying time. If there's anything we can do, just let us know.

Armin and Marjorie said in their letter: "Church had something vital missing Sunday — the Millers!"

Ernie Bauer wrote to us too — on Friday the 13th:

> Glad to hear Rev. Paul is coming along as well as he is. I'd say you were both very lucky to have each other; still, I think in Rev. Paul's case there is Someone a lot more powerful than Lady Luck working for both of you. It's been awhile since I've prayed for anything but since Rev. Paul's accident — well, the only thing *I* could do *was* pray. . . . If anyone's got the right contacts with Him, it's Rev. Paul.

Another young person, Alison Martyn, one of the Youth Center leaders, kept us informed on how things were going. She wrote, among other things:

> We have changed our opening date to January 20. The enthusiasm is really building as things begin to take shape. Our prayers are with you and your family.

Our old friends, the Ford Millers, had moved to California where they had taken the Downey Methodist Church. Ford wrote in prayerful concern:

> I suppose Paul is the best friend I ever had. He is like a brother, and the closest person I have as a brother. God has walked through our lives and through His guidance our relationship has been deeper and more meaningful.

Elma and Vernon Eckel wrote:

> You are feeling better this morning, aren't you? May God keep on with His wonderful healing for your head, body, and soul. Paul, will you please pray for Gene that he might find the right job God wants him to do? . . . I thank God for what I know He is going to do about my prayers for you.

Remember Erma Spellman, who'd mentioned earlier that it would be a miracle if I lived? Well, the first card I wrote after my accident was to Erma, and I signed it: "The Miracle." She sent a card in reply in which she said:

> Dear Paul (The Miracle) . . . all of the hospital staff and doctors ask about you every day — plus all of us who have been praying — God certainly does answer prayers and *miracles* still happen. Your ministry will be blessed by this, I'm sure.

After I had spent several weekends with my family, Miles dashed off a quick note in his own quaint way. He wondered if I'd be able to "take a steady diet of home sweet home." He added:

> Most people thought you'd eaten your last steak about

Dec. 31, right? Isn't it great to have trust and confidence in the Lord Jesus? It's great to be His men!

In an unusual testimonial from Dr. Robert Woods, the neurosurgeon from Menningers, which he wrote some time later, he said:

> The treatment of occasional patients is so unusual that an unforgettable experience is engraved on a doctor's memory. The name Paul Miller will always bring out a chain of memories. From the start I knew he was an unusual person, and the strength of his character supported him through experiences which would have been devastating to most people in this anxious world. Practically all the circumstances related to his injury fit in with the person he is. In the first place, he was helping a group of high schoolers decorate a hall for a New Year's Eve party when a heavy searchlight slipped from the balcony and caused a severe head injury. Within a few days of his operation he was conscious, alert, and cooperative, and one never will see an individual more determined to get well. Considering the severity of the injury to the right side of his head, I could hardly expect that strength or sensation would ever return to any degree on his left side. This was the state in which I transferred him to the Topeka Veteran's Hospital, and yet he made such progress with learning to walk, get around and take care of himself that he was discharged only about six weeks later. When I saw him about two months later he told me he had preached at Easter. By then he was doing all his ministerial work and preaching for two services on Sundays. He has always continued to improve a little between visits each time I have seen him. He represents a good reason for doctors to be careful about forecasting a too gloomy future, even in severe injuries. Faith and courage can surmount unbelievable obstacles.

Unusual concerns for my well-being were expressed

by some of our friends, such as Julie Rundle, who was terribly afraid that her daughter Barbara's visit had been too much for me, for Barb was one of the first people to be admitted to my room, outside of the family.

Julie almost "had a fit," she said, because she worried that the visit was too much for me, and she had prayed that I hadn't been hurt by it.

"Marilyn," she admonished firmly, "please, for Paul's sake, start limiting people! You should have scooted Barb out — after about three minutes!"

Financially, too, we received every consideration. My salary continued, with no questions asked. The chairman of our board of trustees showed up shortly after the first of the year and asked Marilyn for our usual batch of first-or-the-month utility bills and promptly paid them.

While Marilyn's parents, the F. R. Zinns, stayed with the children in Clay Center during those long, uncertain weeks when my life hung in the balance and Marilyn stayed in Topeka, they never lacked for anything. Church friends and neighbors flocked to the parsonage with food until the refrigerator groaned under the supplies that were brought in.

When Leo and Howard, in their concern for our future, began to talk of contacting Social Security officials for my subsequent disability benefits, our Zinn parents were aghast. They never questioned that I wouldn't get well and preach again. Such was their faith!

Organizations and groups held benefits and took up offerings, with the proceeds going into the "Reverend Paul Miller Fund."

Members of the Kiwanis Club served benefit coffees and organized other drives. As the Clay County *Dispatch* stated: "Any civic club or organization interested in having a project to raise money for Rev. Miller, is asked to contact the following Kiwanians — " and listed several names.

(Later this organization purchased a stationary bicycle for me to strengthen my legs. They triggered a project to provide physical therapy equipment for the Clay County Hospital later on also.)

The World Day of Prayer offering on February 10 of that year in Clay Center was designated for the fund. Church circles held food and bake sales; clubs and Sunday school classes, business places, and other community efforts provided vast cash donations, plus scores of other sources which we cannot begin to name.

Hundreds of individuals sent money — some anonymously. One prominent Clay County family and their teenage children gave a considerable amount. Through Dr. Cook's arrangements, the Concordia district of the United Methodist Church paid $700 to Stormont-Vail Hospital.

We heard of another incident which touched us deeply. Gary Melcher, a student from Marion, Kansas, sent in a sizable amount of the money he had earned that summer for college.

"He said he wanted to help, even if he didn't know him," his mother told us.

Marilyn never lacked for a ride to Topeka to visit me, after she was able to go home when I was improving. Someone always offered to bring her the ninety miles. Never did she need to pay out money for a meal during her stay in the capital city. Someone was always there to buy her meals or bring her food.

Even our banker offered to postpone our car payments until we could manage them again.

Howard VonSchriltz' secretary kept the books for all the money that came in and could quote the exact amounts at almost any given hour. Howard was nearly bowled over with amazement at the vast sums that accumulated.

"I think I'll get hit over the head, if it brings in money like that!" he cracked.

Altogether almost $6,000 came in during those nearly three months I spent in the two hospitals. We were completely overwhelmed. Our faith in humanity was bolstered and our spirits humbled as a result of this dynamic show of brotherly love. Later, the insurance company capitulated and came through with some of the money after all.

We haven't begun to mention all of these dear generous people by name, and we cannot thank them enough. Permit us to say it here:

"God bless each one of you for all your love and concern!"

Surely, *it was God!*

6

For some time I had begged the doctors to dismiss me from the hospital and permit me to come in for weekly therapy as an outpatient. Fellow-Kiwanians from Clay Center had arranged to bring me. Since I still wasn't walking too well, I knew the doctors would deliberate a good while before giving their final word.

The last wonderful weekend I had spent at home made it all the more miserable for me to return to the disheartening sights of Ward I-5A.

Marilyn, sensing my reluctance to return, wrote to me the very day I left to go back to Topeka. Her words were like fresh cold water to a thirsty house-plant. She wrote:

> Decided to write you right away as I know how you hated to have to go back to the hospital again. Sure hope you had a good ride and didn't get sick over it. Enjoyed our time together so much it was kind of like a dream you can't stand to have end. But feel sure that it is God's will that you have this time down there to get your strength back and the therapy too. So will try to be mature and stick it out until you are well and out of there for good. I love you so much and enjoy your company. Sorry the kids bothered you but realize your nerves have had a blow, too, so can understand that. . . .
>
> I'm anxious to come down now and talk to the doctors about how soon you can come home as an outpatient. I felt you've really done so well while you

were home and it surely won't be long until you can be up and out again. I'm real proud of the way you are so determined to get well. Some men would use this as a chance not to get back to work, but not my wonderful husband. . . . I will pray with you about the doctors letting you be an outpatient. We've had so many answers to prayers that certainly God will work it out if He sees fit that you should be at home instead of there. . . ."

Dear, wonderful Marilyn . . . so patient and kind and understanding . . . What would I do without you? . . . I need you, my darling . . .I love you. . . . The tears fell as I finished reading her letter.

Experience had proved that each time I had been home I seemed better, and so after a lengthy consultation the doctors agreed I could go home.

I had attended worship service at the Ebenezer church on two weekends while home, and I almost cried as I listened to Glenn Claycamp preach. I appreciated Glenn's help, of course, but I wanted so badly to be in the pulpit again.

"It's going to be hard, Paul Miller," I told myself firmly. "You know you still can't navigate too well on your own; and talking still gives you trouble. Even your eyesight bothers you. Think you can make it?"

I couldn't do it in my own strength, but in *God* I could. And on March 20, 1967, I sat waiting impatiently, clutching my release papers when Harold and Gladys Trumpp drove to Topeka with Marilyn to get me.

The raw March wind bit sharply through my coat as I stumbled down the curb and got into the car. The ninety-mile drive to Clay Center seemed endless and unreal. It was as though I had come out of a prison and the gates had clanged shut behind me. From now on I would be free!

After I got home, Howard drove me downtown for coffee. I had to stop and greet my friends and parishioners along the way. I think I laughed and joked more that day than at any time in my life. It was great to be back home.

Two men came over one day and suggested that I sue the city for $250,000 because of the spotlight which caused my accident.

I shook my still-bandaged head. "No. I'd rather have friends and walk up and down Clay Center's streets with my head up than all the filthy lucre which can't pay for the months of agonizing pain and frustration anyhow."

When the Clay Center Jaycees held their annual awards banquet I was one of four men to receive special recognition.

"Paul Miller has been a winner in two ways," said President John Smith of the Jaycees. "He has won the respect of the people in working on community projects, and because he has learned the ability of giving of his life to God and to man to help make this a better world to live in. He made special efforts in helping promote the youth center. Clay County should be proud of this man."

Easter Sunday came on March 26. The day was cold but the sky, a pale, eggshell-rinsed blue, stretched over the barren landscape. Excitement budded along my spine as I struggled into my best suit.

"It doesn't bag very much," I jibed as I stood before the mirror. "Does it?"

Marilyn's eyes shone. "You look fine to me, Paul. Absolutely wonderful."

After a pause she looked at me tenderly and continued: "You're sure conducting two services today won't be too much for you?"

I adjusted my tie carefully. "Earl is assisting me at Hayes and Arvin at Ebenezer. Besides, Ebenezer even suggested I sit down to preach, if it would be easier."

"What did you tell them?"

For a minute I toyed with the tie until I had it

Clay Center, Kansas, Jaycees President John Smith presenting Paul D. Miller with Distinguished Service Award in 1967.

straight. "I've never sat down while preaching yet and I don't aim to start now!"

We drove the nine miles to the Hayes church where I was to preach at 9:30. The white frame country church was silhouetted against the bright morning sky and it seemed bathed in a special Easter glow just for me.

After we pulled up to the door I stepped out of the car with mixed feelings. One of my laymen, Earl Grumme, helped me through the door. The quiet murmur of voices hushed as I walked slowly toward the pulpit, leaning on my cane. Earl helped me up

The First Methodist Church, Peabody, Kansas, of which Paul D. Miller is pastor. Photo by Howard O'Neal.

194

the steps to the platform. I had made it a practice to kneel briefly to pray before conducting the service but of course, I couldn't now. I sat down while Earl took charge of the service.

Then I arose to preach. Almost three months had passed since I had stood before either of my two congregations, and it wasn't easy now. I knew I still looked haggard from weeks of suffering, and my mouth was drawn up sharply on the left side. I couldn't use my arms for my customary motions, and I blinked my eyes, trying to focus them in front of me. For a moment I froze. How would the people respond to

Paul D. Miller family, December 1970. From left to right: Kassie, Marilyn, Krassina, Paul, Vincent, and Kay Lani.

one who looked as inhuman as I?

As I glanced over my congregation I saw love, compassion, courage, concern, gratefulness, and joy mingled on their faces, and it gave me the leverage I needed. A great weight lifted from me, and joy welled over me like a newly opened fountain. The experience superseded the first time I stood behind the Broughton pulpit.

I opened my Bible and from my sermon notes I read my text.

I reread the beautiful story of the empty tomb and the risen Christ. I told them of the women who had come to the sepulcher, seeking Jesus, and how the angel had said to them:

"Ye seek Jesus of Nazareth, which was crucified: he is risen; he is not here; behold the place where they laid him."

I went on to tell them of the abundant life which is ours through His resurrection and how we too can be made alive through Him. In some way I too had "risen" from the bitterness of poverty and degradation, pain and despair, to a life of service for Him. More recently I had risen from what some had predicted — physical death.

At the close of the service I pronounced the benediction which St. Francis of Assissi had handed down to us through the ages:

Lord, make me an instrument of Your peace. Where there is hatred, let me sow love; where there is injury, pardon; where there is doubt, faith; where there is despair, hope; where there is darkness, light; and where there is sadness, joy. . . . Grant that I may seek to console; to understand; to love. For it is in giving that we receive; pardoning that we are pardoned; dying that we are born to eternal life.

After the "amen" I staggered down the aisle and through the door. Marilyn helped me into the car and we began our drive to the Ebenezer church for the 10:45 service, with a repeat sermon.

"How'd I do?" I blurted suddenly after we had driven in silence for several miles.

Marilyn's brown eyes lit up with love and understanding. "You were wonderful, Paul. You were relying on our motto — I'm sure you were."

"I can do all things through Christ which strengtheneth me." Why, of course! This is why I had been able to walk again — because He was providing the strength for my imperfect body. He also knew I had "miles to go" before my service for Him would be ended, for He still had plans for me.

When we arrived at the Ebenezer church I knew Arvin Hoffman would assist me, as Earl had done at Hayes, and that there was nothing to fear. During the service the great Epiphany hymn, "Go, Tell It on the Mountain," swelled from the throats and hearts of the congregation and I joined in heartily. Even though the hymn was out of season, I had chosen it because it too spoke of "go — and tell."

As I started my halting footsteps toward the pulpit, I remembered the reassuring pressure of Marilyn's fingers on mine, and her words:

"Ditto, Paul. . . ."

"Ditto," I whispered softly, and once more I opened my Bible to tell of God's love.

197

The Authors

Esther L. Vogt was born at Collinsville, Oklahoma. At the age of eight she with her parents moved to a Kansas farm where she grew up. Since then she has lived in Kansas.

She graduated from Tabor College, Hillsboro, Kansas, in 1939 with majors in English and elementary education. She then taught school for three years.

In 1942 she was married to Curt Vogt. They have three grown chil-

Paul D. Miller is presently pastor of the Peabody-Summit churches, Marion County, Kansas, with a membership of 399. He is active in civic affairs serving as a member of the Peabody Local Housing Authority, the Advisory Board of the Peabody Memorial Nursing Home, the Peabody Centennial Committee, the Board of Directors of the Peabody Chamber of Commerce, Trustee of the Conference Pension En-

198

dien. They now live in Hillsboro, Kansas, and are members of the Hillsboro Mennonite Brethren Church.

She has always had a desire to write and has written nearly 500 short stories and four novels of book length, *Cry to the Wind, The Sky Is Falling, High Ground,* and *Ann.* She is a member of the Kansas Authors Club and has served two years as president of the fourth district. Her hobbies are piano playing and reading.

dowment Fund, President of the Peabody Association of Churches, and a member of the District Stewardship Committee.

I'LL WALK AGAIN

I'LL WALK AGAIN is an exciting in-depth story about Reverend Paul D. Miller. His story, his life, his accident, and his literal resurrection are proof that miracles do occur in the twentieth century.

Today in Peabody, Kansas, Reverend Miller is a Methodist minister, but only four years ago his life was shattered by a tragic accident that rendered him completely immobile, never to walk or preach again. This setback did not deter Reverend Miller. He stated that on Easter Sunday he would be in his pulpit and preach the Resurrection. Through the grace of God that is what he did.

This is a story of a miracle, the miracle of God's grace through Jesus Christ.